Editor
Sara Connolly

Managing Editor
Ina Massler Levin, M.A.

Illustrator
Kevin McCarthy

Cover Artist
Brenda DiAntonis

Art Production Manager
Kevin Barnes

Imaging
James Edward Grace
Rosa C. See

Publisher
Mary D. Smith, M.S. Ed.

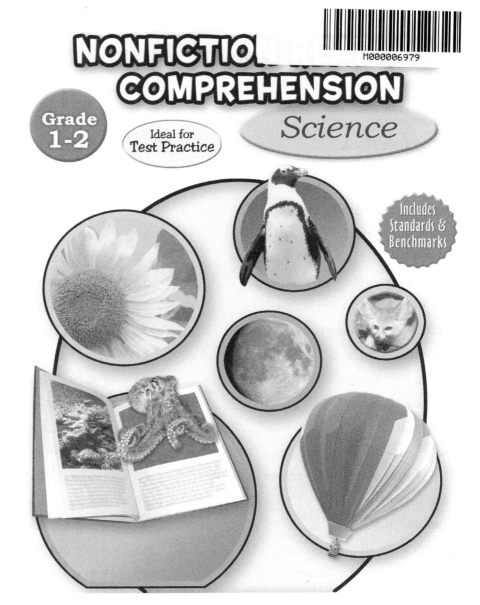

NONFICTION
COMPREHENSION
Science

Grade 1-2

Ideal for **Test Practice**

Includes Standards & Benchmarks

Author

Ruth Foster, M.Ed.

Teacher Created Resources

Teacher Created Resources, Inc.
12621 Western Avenue
Garden Grove, CA 92841
www.teachercreated.com
ISBN: 978-1-4206-8026-3
©2006 Teacher Created Resources, Inc.
Reprinted, 2019
Made in U.S.A.

Table of Contents

Introduction

> ❊ **Science is thrilling.**
>   A waterspout once caused it to rain toads in France!
>
> ❊ **It has changed our world.**
>   Think of Morgan's invention of the gas mask.
>
> ❊ **It affects our lives daily.**
>   Think of how we use steel to make tools and construct buildings.

Reading comprehension can be practiced and improved while coupled with science instruction. This book presents short, fascinating science stories. The stories were chosen to incite curiosity, augment basic science facts taught at this grade level, and introduce a world of ideas, people, and animals.

A page of questions follows each story. These questions will provide a child familiarity with different types of test questions. In addition, the practice they provide will help a child develop good testing skills. Questions are written so that they lead a child to focus on what was read. They provide practice for finding the main idea as well as specific details. They provide practice in deciphering new and unknown vocabulary words. In addition, the questions encourage a child to think beyond the facts. For example, every question set has an analogy question where students are expected to think about the relationship between two things and find a pair of words with the same type of relationship. Other questions provide an opportunity for the child to extrapolate and consider possible consequences relevant to the information provided in the story.

The book is written so that writing can be incorporated into every lesson. The level of writing will depend on what the teacher desires, as well as the needs of the child.

Lessons in *Nonfiction Reading Comprehension: Science* meet and are correlated to the Mid-continent Research for Education and Learning (McRel) standards. They are listed on page 8.

A place for *Nonfiction Reading Comprehension: Science* can be found in every classroom or home. It can be a part of daily instruction in time designated for both reading and science. It can be used for both group and individual instruction. Stories can be read with someone or on ones own. *Nonfiction Reading Comprehension: Science* can help children improve in multiple areas, including reading, science, critical thinking, writing, and test-taking.

Using This Book

The Stories

Each story in *Nonfiction Reading Comprehension: Science* is a separate unit. For this reason, the stories can but do not have to be read in order. A teacher can choose any story that matches classroom activity.

Stories can be assigned to be read during either science or reading periods. They can be used as classroom work or as supplemental material.

Each story is five paragraphs long. They range from 275 to 300 words long. They are written at grade level with elementary sentence structure.

New Words

Each story is provided with a list of eight new words. Each of the new words is used a minimum of two times in the story. New words may sometimes have an addition of a simple word ending such as "s," "ed," or "ing." The new words are introduced in the story in the same order that they are presented in the new word list. Many of the new words are found in more than one story. Mastery of the new words may not come immediately, but practice articulating, seeing, and writing the words will build a foundation for future learning.

- A teacher may choose to have the children read and repeat the words together as a class.

- While it is true that the majority of the words are defined explicitly or in context in the stories, a teacher may choose to discuss and define the new words before the children start reading. This will only reinforce sight word identification and reading vocabulary.

- A teacher may engage the class in an activity where children use the new word in a sentence. Or, the teacher may use the word in two sentences. Only one sentence will use the word correctly. Children will be asked to identify which sentence is correct. For example, one new word is *teeth*. The teacher might say,

  "You chew your food with your teeth."

  "You use your teeth to see."

- A teacher may also allow children to choose one new word to add to their weekly spelling list. This provides children with an opportunity to feel part of a decision-making process, as well as to gain "ownership" over new words.

In addition, practice spelling sight words reinforces the idea that we can learn to recognize new words across stories because there is consistency in spelling.

- A teacher may choose to have children go through the story after it is read and circle each new word one or two times.

Using This Book *(cont.)*

The Writing Link

A teacher may choose to link writing exercises to the science stories presented in the book. All writing links reinforce handwriting and spelling skills. Writing links with optional sentence tasks reinforce sentence construction and punctuation.

✳ A teacher may choose to have a child pick one new word from the list of new words and write it out. Space for the word write-out is provided in this book. This option may seem simple, but it provides a child with an opportunity to take control. The child is not overwhelmed by the task of the word write-out because the child is choosing the word. It also reinforces sight-word identification. If a teacher has begun to instruct children in cursive writing, the teacher can ask the child to write out the word twice, once in print, and once in cursive.

✳ A teacher may choose to have a child write out a complete sentence using one of the new words. The sentences can by formulated together as a class, or as individual work. Depending on other classroom work, the teacher may want to remind children about capital letters and ending punctuation.

✳ A teacher may require a child to write out a sentence after the story questions have been answered. The sentence may or may not contain a new word. The sentence may have one of the following starts:

- I learned . . .
- I thought . . .

- Did you know . . .
- An interesting thing about . . .

If the teacher decides on this type of sentence formation, the teacher may want to show children how they can use words directly from the story to help form their sentences, as well as make sure that words in their sentences are not misspelled. For example, this is the first paragraph in the selection titled "Sharks."

How many teeth do you have? How many teeth have you lost? A shark has lots more teeth than you. Some sharks have hundreds of teeth. Sharks lose more teeth than you, too. In fact, sharks lose their teeth all the time. Feel your teeth. They are set firmly into your jaw. When something is firmly set, it does not move. It is fixed. A shark's teeth are not firmly set.

Possible sample sentence write-outs may be

"I learned that sharks have lots of teeth."

"I thought sharks didn't lose teeth."

"Did you know that sharks have hundreds of teeth?"

"An interesting thing about a shark is that it has more teeth than you."

The Writing Link *(cont.)*

This type of exercise reinforces spelling and sentence structure. It also teaches a child responsibility—a child learns to go back to the story to check word spelling. It also provides elementary report writing skills. Students are taking information from a story source and reporting it in their own sentence construction.

The Questions

Five questions follow every story. Questions always contain one main idea, specific detail, and analogy question.

* The main idea question pushes a child to focus on the topic of what was read. It allows practice in discerning between answers that are too broad or narrow.

* The specific detail question requires a child to retrieve or recall a particular fact mentioned in the story. Children gain practice referring back to a source. They also are pushed to think about the structure of the story. Where would this fact most likely be mentioned in the story? What paragraph would most likely contain the fact they are retrieving?

* The analogy question pushes a child to develop reasoning skills. It pairs two words mentioned in the story and asks the child to think about how the words relate to each other. A child is then asked to find an analogous pair. Children are expected to recognize and use analogies in all course readings, written work, and listening. This particular type of question is found on many cognitive-functioning tests.

* The remaining two questions are a mixture of vocabulary, inference, or sequencing questions. Going back and reading the word in context can always answer vocabulary questions. The inference and sequencing questions provide practice for what students will find on standardized tests. They also encourage a child to think beyond the story. They push a child to think critically about how facts can be interpreted or why something works.

The Test Link

Standardized tests have become obligatory in schools throughout our nation and the world. There are certain test-taking skills and strategies that can be developed by using *Nonfiction Reading Comprehension: Science.*

* Questions can be answered on the page by filling in the bubble, or the questions can be answered by having students fill in the appropriate bubble pages on page 141. Filling in the bubble pages provides practice responding in a standardized-test format.

* Questions are presented in a mixed up order, though the main-idea question is always amoung the first three. The analogy question is always one of the last three. This mixed up order provides practice with standardized test formats, where though reading comprehension passages often have main-idea questions, the main idea question is not necessarily placed first.

The Test Link (cont.)

✳ A teacher may want to point out to students that often a main idea question can be used to help a child focus on what the story is about. A teacher may also want to point out that an analogy question can be done any time, as it is not crucial to the main focus of the story.

✳ A teacher may want to reinforce that a child should read every answer choice. Many children are afraid of not remembering information. Reinforcing this tip helps a child to remember that on multiple-choice tests, one is *identifying* the best answer, not making an answer up.

✳ A teacher may choose to discuss the strategy of eliminating wrong answer choices to find the correct one. Teachers should instruct children that even if they can only eliminate one answer choice, their guess will have a better chance of being right. A teacher may want to go through several questions to demonstrate this strategy. For example, in the "Sharks" selection, there is the question:

1. This story is mainly about

ⓐ eggs   ⓒ teeth

ⓑ pups   ⓓ sharks

Although eggs, teeth, and sharks are mentioned in the story, there is no mention of pups. A child may be able to eliminate that answer choice immediately. A guess at this point has a better change of being correct than when there were four choices to choose from. A teacher can remind children, too, that there is the option of going back and finding the paragraphs with the words *eggs*, *teeth*, and *sharks* in them. Sharks are mentioned in all paragraphs, where as eggs and teeth are separate topics. In fact, they appear to have equal weight. As one cannot be a better choice than the other, neither one of them can be correct.

The Thrill of Science

The challenge in writing this book was to allow a child access to the thrills of science while understanding that many science words or concepts are beyond a child's elementary grade level. It is hoped that the range of stories and the ways concepts are presented reinforces basic science concepts, all while improving basic reading comprehension skills. It is also hoped that a child's imagination is whetted. After reading each story, a child will want to question and find out more.

Meeting Standards

Listed below are the McREL standards for language arts Level 1 (grades K–2). All standards and benchmarks are used with permission from McREL:

Copyright 2004 McREL

Mid-continent Research for Education and Learning

2550 S. Parker Road, Suite 500

Aurora, CO 80014

Telephone: (303) 337-0990

Website: *www.mcrel.org/standards-benchmarks*

McREL Standards are in **bold**. Benchmarks are in regular print. All lessons meet the following standards and benchmarks unless noted.

Uses grammatical and mechanical conventions in written compositions.

- Uses conventions of print in writing (all lessons where writing a new word or sentence option is followed)

- Uses complete sentences in written compositions (all lessons where writing a complete sentence option is followed)

Uses the general skills and strategies of the reading process.

- Understands that print conveys meaning
- Understands how print is organized and read
- Creates mental images from pictures and print
- Uses meaning clues
- Uses basic elements of phonetic analysis
- Uses basic elements of structural analysis
- Understands level-appropriate sight words and vocabulary
- Uses self-correction strategies

Uses reading skills and strategies to understand a variety of informational texts.

- Uses reading skills and strategies to understand a variety of informational texts
- Understands the main idea and supporting details of simple expository information

Sharks

These are new words to practice.

Say each word 10 times.

✳ teeth	✳ hatched
✳ shark	✳ thick
✳ firmly	✳ rubbery
✳ jaw	✳ strings

Choose one new word to write.

_____

\- -

_____

Sharks

How many teeth do you have? How many teeth have you lost? A shark has lots more teeth than you. Some sharks have hundreds of teeth. Sharks lose more teeth than you, too. In fact, sharks lose their teeth all the time. Feel your teeth. They are set firmly into your jaw. When something is firmly set, it does not move. It is fixed. A shark's teeth are not firmly set.

Sharks have sharp teeth. Sharp teeth are good for cutting. Sharks can bite down hard. Some sharks bite down so hard that their teeth can cut through steel! Every time a shark bites down hard it may lose a tooth. This is because the teeth are not firmly fixed in the shark's jaw. Most sharks eat meat. They use their sharp teeth to cut up their meat.

Losing a tooth does not bother a shark. Why not? Sharks have many new teeth. The new teeth are in the jaws. The new teeth come out fast. How fast? It takes only 24 hours for some teeth to grow in. A shark can have new teeth in just one day!

Most sharks are born alive. They are born ready to hunt. Nurse sharks have about 20 to 30 babies at a time. Nurse shark babies are about one foot (30 centimeters) long when they are born. Great White shark babies are bigger. Some Great White babies are four-and-one-half feet (137 centimeters) long!

Other sharks are hatched. They are hatched out of eggs. The eggs are not hard. The eggs are thick. They are rubbery. The thick rubbery eggs protect the babies inside. Most of the eggs have strings on them. The strings catch on seaweed. The strings catch on coral. They keep the eggs from floating away.

Sharks

After reading the story, answer the questions.
Fill in the circle next to the correct answer.

1. This story is mainly about

   (a) eggs
   (b) pups
   (c) teeth
   (d) sharks

2. Why are shark eggs thick and rubbery?

   (a) to catch on seaweed
   (b) to firmly fix strings
   (c) to protect the babies inside
   (d) to keep the eggs from floating away

3. Think about how the word **tooth** relates to **teeth**. Which words relate in the same way?

tooth : teeth

   (a) babies : baby
   (b) shark : sharks
   (c) eggs : strings
   (d) seaweed : coral

4. From the story you can tell that

   (a) all sharks are born alive
   (b) one baby shark is born at a time
   (c) there is more than one kind of shark
   (d) it takes a long time for shark teeth to grow in

5. When something is firm, it

   (a) does not move
   (b) is thick and rubbery
   (c) grows back in 24 hours
   (d) needs strings to keep from floating

Something Fast

These are new words to practice.

Say each word 10 times.

✳ sneeze	✳ floating
✳ rushes	✳ specks
✳ lungs	✳ mucus
✳ tiny	✳ irritates

Choose one new word to write.

_____

- -

_____

Something Fast

"I do something fast," said Sam. "I do it faster than I can run. I do it faster than I can swim. I do it faster than I can ride my bike. I do it as fast as a car. I do it at 70 miles (110 kilometers) per hour. You do it, too." What can Sam do? What can you do, too?

Sam can sneeze. When you sneeze, air rushes down your nose. The air comes from your lungs. It rushes fast. It rushes faster than you can run. It rushes faster than you can swim. It rushes faster than you can ride a bike. It rushes as fast as a car. It rushes at 70 miles (110 kilometers) per hour.

Air is made out of gases. Tiny things are in air. The tiny things are too small to see. They float in the air. Some of the floating things are specks of dirt. Some of the floating things are germs. Germs are tiny forms of life. Germs can make you sick. When you breathe in, you take in air. You take in gas. You take in dirt and germs, too.

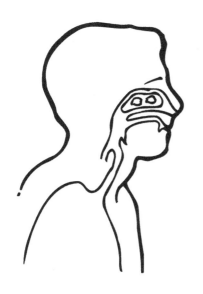

We have a trap in our nose. The trap protects the skin inside our nose. The trap is a layer of mucus. Mucus is like slime. It coats the inside of parts of our body. Our nose mucus traps dirt. It traps germs.

Sometimes a tiny speck irritates the inside of our nose. When something is irritated, it is bothered. The inside of our nose begins to itch. It begins to tingle. It makes us sneeze. The sneeze is a jet of air. It comes from our lungs. It goes down our nose. It sweeps mucus and irritating specks. It sweeps them out of our nose.

Something Fast

After reading the story, answer the questions.
Fill in the circle next to the correct answer.

1. What is the trap inside our nose made of?

   (a) germs

   (b) mucus

   (c) lungs

   (d) gases

2. What statement is true about when we sneeze?

   (a) We sweep mucus into our nose.

   (b) We sweep tiny germs into our nose.

   (c) Air rushes from our nose down our lungs.

   (d) Air rushes from our lungs down our nose.

3. This story is mainly about

   (a) Sam

   (b) germs

   (c) sneezing

   (d) tiny specks

4. Cats bother Sam. Cats make Sam sneeze. Sam is _____ by cats.

   (a) rushed

   (b) trapped

   (c) protected

   (d) irritated

5. Think about how the word **speck** relates to **tiny**. Which words relate in the same way?

speck : tiny

   (a) dirt : air

   (b) ride : bike

   (c) germ : small

   (d) lungs : nose

The First Step on the Moon

These are new words to practice.
Say each word 10 times.

* spacesuit   * special

* lunar   * scientists

* soil   * craters

* pocket   * mountains

Choose one new word to write.

The First Step on the Moon

The day was July 20th. The year was 1969. Neil Armstrong stepped out. He stepped out onto the moon. It had taken him three days to get there. He had to wear a spacesuit. He had to wear a suit because there was no air on the moon. There was no water. No one had ever gone to the moon before. Neil was the first man on the moon.

Neil did something. He did it right away. He did it as soon as he stepped out. What did Neil do? He took some lunar soil. Lunar soil is ground. It is ground from the moon. Lunar soil is rocky. It is dusty. Neil put the lunar soil in a bag. He put the bag in a pocket. The pocket was special. It was in his spacesuit. It was made just for the lunar soil.

Why did Neil take lunar soil? Why did he put it in a special pocket? No one had ever been to the moon before. Scientists did not know what would happen. What if Neil had to leave the moon fast? What if Neil had to leave before he could find out things for the scientists? Neil picked up the soil first. He did it so that if he had to come back fast, he would not be empty-handed. Scientists could look at the rocks. They could study them. They could learn about the moon.

The moon has lots of craters. Craters are holes. The holes are shaped like bowls. Some craters are small. Some craters are big. One crater is so big that a city the size of London could fit in it! Mountains are on the moon, too. One mountain is very high. It is almost as high as the highest mountain on Earth.

The First Step on the Moon

After reading the story, answer the questions.
Fill in the circle next to the correct answer.

1. This story is mainly about

   (a) big and small craters
   (b) scientists and lunar soil
   (c) Neil Armstrong and the moon
   (d) a special pocket on Neil's spacesuit

2. How long did it take Neil to get to the moon?

   (a) one day
   (b) 20 years
   (c) three days
   (d) 1969 years

3. Think about how the word **mountain** relates to **high**. Which words relate in the same way?

   > **mountain : high**

   (a) step : out
   (b) rock : pocket
   (c) spacesuit : air
   (d) crater : bowl-shaped

4. What is not true about craters?

   (a) They are high.
   (b) They are holes.
   (c) They are big and small.
   (d) They are shaped like bowls.

5. What answer is in the right order?

   (a) Neil put on a spacesuit; Neil got soil; Neil stepped out.
   (b) Neil stepped out; Neil got soil; Neil put soil in his pocket.
   (c) Neil went to the moon; Neil stepped out; Neil put on a spacesuit.
   (d) Neil put soil in his pocket; Neil stepped out; Neil went to the moon.

Eating Without Teeth

These are new words to practice.
Say each word 10 times.

✳ teeth	✳ hollow
✳ skeleton	✳ proboscis
✳ exoskeleton	✳ squirts
✳ tube	✳ juice

Choose one new word to write.

_____

- -

_____

Eating Without Teeth

A fly does not have teeth. A fly cannot bite. A fly cannot chew food. How can a fly eat? How can it eat without teeth? How can it eat without biting? How can it eat without chewing?

All flies are insects. They are light. They are light because they do not have any bones. You have bones. Your bones are heavy. They are inside you. They make up your skeleton. Insects do not have inside skeletons. They have exoskeletons. Exoskeletons are on the outside. They are like hard shells. They keep the soft insides safe.

A fly has a long tube. The tube is hollow. The tube is called a proboscis. When a fly wants to eat, it lowers its proboscis. A fly cannot eat hard food. It cannot chew. It can only drink. It sucks up food with its proboscis. The food goes up the hollow tube. The fly sucks it up.

What if a fly wants to eat something hard? What if a fly wants to eat sugar? The fly lowers its proboscis. It squirts juice. It squirts it onto the sugar. The juice does something. The juice makes the sugar soft. It makes it so the sugar can be sucked up. The sugar can be sucked up the proboscis. It can go up the hollow tube.

How does a fly know what to eat? Can a fly taste food? A fly tastes with its feet. A fly has hair on its feet. The hairs are special. The hairs taste the food. The hairs feel if the food is hot. They feel if the food is cold. When a fly is walking on your food, it is doing more than just walking. It is tasting, too!

Eating Without Teeth

After reading the story, answer the questions.
Fill in the circle next to the correct answer.

1. If a fly wanted to eat rice or bread, it would have to
   - (a) first chew it lightly
   - (b) first suck it up with its proboscis
   - (c) first walk on it to see if it was hot
   - (d) first squirt juice on it so it could drink it

2. This story is mainly about
   - (a) flies
   - (b) insects
   - (c) tasting
   - (d) hollow tubes

3. How does a fly taste food?
   - (a) It lowers its proboscis.
   - (b) It uses its exoskeleton.
   - (c) It uses special hair on its feet.
   - (d) It squirts juice onto what it wants to eat.

4. What statement is true?
   - (a) Some flies have teeth.
   - (b) All flies are insects.
   - (c) All insects are flies.
   - (d) Some flies are insects.

5. Think about how the word **inside** relates to **outside**. Which words relate in the same way?

   | inside : outside |

   - (a) fly : insect
   - (b) insect : fly
   - (c) exoskeleton : skeleton
   - (d) skeleton : exoskeleton

All About Wind

These are new words to practice.

Say each word 10 times.

* gentle	* pilots
* gale	* trade
* pattern	* steady
* streams	* westward

Choose one new word to write.

_____

- -

_____

All About Wind

Air is all around us. The air around us is made of gas. Gas is not a solid. Gas is not a liquid. Air is made up of different gases. You cannot see the air around us. How do you know there is air? Sometimes you can feel air. Air moves all the time. Sometimes air moves slowly. Sometimes air moves fast. When air moves fast enough for you to feel, it is called wind. Wind is moving air.

Some winds are light. They are gentle winds. Light, gentle winds are called breezes. Some winds are strong. Very strong winds are gales. Gale winds can blow down trees. Gale winds can blow down houses.

Some winds are part of a pattern. The pattern is big. The pattern covers Earth. The pattern is a way of acting. The way of acting does not change. What makes the patterns? The sun's heat makes the patterns. The way the Earth turns make the patterns.

Jet streams are high. They are high above the Earth. Jet streams go around Earth from west to east. Airline pilots try to fly along with jet streams. Why do pilots want to fly along with jet streams? Jet streams are strong. They are so strong that they can help a pilot go fast. A pilot can save many hours by flying with the jet stream.

Sailors know about wind patterns, too. Sailors do not use jet streams. They use the trade winds. Trade winds blow close to the surface of the Earth. Trade winds are a steady wind. When something is steady, it does not let up. It does not change. Trade winds blow toward the equator. They blow westward. Sailors named the trade winds. Sailors use the trade winds when they make westward ocean crossings.

All About Wind

After reading the story, answer the questions.
Fill in the circle next to the correct answer.

1. This story is mainly about

   (a) breezes
   (b) the jet stream
   (c) fast moving air
   (d) the trade winds

2. Trade winds

   (a) are steady winds.
   (b) are slow moving gases.
   (c) are used by airline pilots.
   (d) blow down trees and houses.

3. Think about how the word **strong** relates to **gentle**. Which words relate in the same way?

   | **strong : gentle** |

   (a) air : gas
   (b) blow : wind
   (c) gale : breeze
   (d) sailor : ocean

4. One reason sailors might not use the jet stream is because

   (a) the jet stream is high up.
   (b) the jet stream is not steady.
   (c) the jet stream is not strong.
   (d) the jet stream blows close to the equator.

5. What makes some winds part of a pattern?

   (a) fast moving gases and the ocean
   (b) the way Earth turns and the ocean
   (c) the sun's heat and fast-moving gases
   (d) the sun's heat and the way Earth turns

Seeds with Wings and Other Things

These are new words to practice.

Say each word 10 times.

* stuck   * overcrowded

* different   * hooks

* coconut   * travel

* spread   * fruit

Choose one new word to write.

_____

- -

_____

Seeds with Wings and Other Things

Ann had a dog. Its fur was a mess. Things were stuck to the dog's fur. Ann had to brush her dog. She had to pick out the things in the fur. "I do not mind," said Ann. "I can pick out the stuck things. My dog is only helping plants grow." Could Ann be right? Could things stuck in dog fur help plants grow?

Plants grow from seeds. Different plants have different kinds of seeds. Some seeds are big. A coconut is a seed. Some coconut seeds weigh 40 pounds (18 kilograms)! Some seeds are small. Orchids are flowers. Some orchid seeds are as small as dust!

A plant tries to spread its seeds. What if the seeds did not spread? What if the seeds just dropped? Too many plants would grow in one place. The plants would be overcrowded. Plants grow better when they are not overcrowded. Seeds spread in different ways. Some seeds have hooks. Some seeds have spines. The seeds get hooked on fur. The seeds get stuck in skin. The seeds travel on fur or in skin. The seeds travel far away.

Ann's dog's fur was a mess. It was a mess because it had things stuck to it. The things were seeds! The seeds were traveling on Ann's dog. When the seeds fell off, they could grow. They could grow in a new place.

Some seeds have very big hooks. The hooks stick to elephants! They hook to the bottom of elephant's feet!

Some seeds are in fruit. Animals eat the fruit. They drop the fruit seeds away from the plant. Other seeds have wings. The wind blows. It blows the winged seeds far away. Some seeds float on the wind. The seeds are light. They have little hairs. They float far away.

Seeds with Wings and Other Things

**After reading the story, answer the questions.
Fill in the circle next to the correct answer.**

1. How did Ann think her dog could help plants grow?

   ⓐ by eating seeds

   ⓑ by being brushed

   ⓒ by spreading seeds

   ⓓ by having messy fur

2. If you saw something floating in the air, it might be

   ⓐ a coconut

   ⓑ a fruit seed

   ⓒ a seeds with hooks

   ⓓ a seed with little hairs

3. This story is mainly about

   ⓐ Ann's dog

   ⓑ how seeds spread

   ⓒ the biggest seed

   ⓓ seeds with hooks

4. When something travels, it

   ⓐ has hooks

   ⓑ is overcrowded

   ⓒ stays in one place

   ⓓ goes from one place to another

5. Think about how the word **bird** relates to **eggs**. Which words relate in the same way?

bird : eggs

   ⓐ dog : fur

   ⓑ plant : seeds

   ⓒ coconuts : big

   ⓓ travel : floats

Steel

These are new words to practice.

Say each word 10 times.

✳ steel	✳ ore
✳ bridges	✳ mine
✳ metal	✳ liquid
✳ iron	✳ oxygen

Choose one new word to write.

_____

- -

_____

Steel

Steel is strong. Steel is light. We make many things out of steel. Bridges need to be strong and light. We make bridges out of steel. We use steel in tall buildings. The strong, light steel helps hold up the building. We use steel in cars. We make tools out of steel. We make pots and pans. We make spoons and knives. We use steel every day. We use it for many things.

Where do we get steel? Is it a plant? Is it a rock? Steel is not a plant. We cannot grow steel. It is not alive. Steel is not a rock. We cannot just find it. We have to make it.

Steel is a metal. It is a special metal. We make it from iron. Iron is a metal. Iron is found in a rock called iron ore. We mine iron ore. When we mine something, we dig it out.

The iron ore is sent to a steel plant. The steel plant has big ovens. Some ovens are used to heat the iron ore. The ovens get very hot. They get so hot that the iron ore melts. It turns from a solid into a liquid. The liquid iron is poured into more ovens. These ovens blow oxygen through the melted iron. The oxygen burns out everything but the iron.

The iron is changed to steel. We mix things into the melted iron. When we add different things, we make different kinds of steel. What do we do with the hot steel? We pour some steel into molds. We form it into blocks. We pass some steel between rollers. The rollers shape the steel into flat pieces. We can make things from the blocks. We can make things from the flat pieces.

Steel

After reading the story, answer the questions.
Fill in the circle next to the correct answer.

1. Which statement is true?

   ⓐ We can mine steel.

   ⓑ We can grow steel.

   ⓒ Steel is made from iron.

   ⓓ Steel is made from blocks and flat pieces.

2. This story is mainly about

   ⓐ metal

   ⓑ steel

   ⓒ bridges

   ⓓ iron ore

3. Which answer is in the correct order?

   ⓐ mine iron ore, melt it, pour steel into molds

   ⓑ mine iron ore, melt it, send it to a steel plant

   ⓒ send iron ore to a steel plant, melt it, mine it

   ⓓ send iron ore to a steel plant, pour steel into molds, melt it

4. What do some ovens blow through the melted iron?

   ⓐ metal

   ⓑ oxygen

   ⓒ rollers

   ⓓ iron ore

5. Think about how the word **iron** relates to **metal**. Which words relate in the same way?

iron : metal

   ⓐ steel : solid

   ⓑ steel : liquid

   ⓒ iron ore : mine

   ⓓ iron ore : rock

Animal Tricks

These are new words to practice.

Say each word 10 times.

* worm   * anglerfish

* wiggles   * glows

* mouth   * insect

* ocean   * mimics

Choose one new word to write.

_____

- -

_____

Animal Tricks

A fish sees a worm. The worm is pink. It wiggles. The fish wants to eat the worm. It swims to the worm. Snap! A mouth bites down. Something is eaten. It is not the worm that is eaten! It is the fish! The worm is not a worm. The worm is the pink tip of a snapping turtle's tongue. The turtle wiggles its tongue. It tricks fish with its pink tip.

One fish lives in the ocean. It is an anglerfish. The anglerfish lives deep down in the water. It is very dark deep down in the ocean. The anglerfish has a "fishing line." The "fishing line" is part of the fish. It hangs over the fish's mouth. The end of the line glows. When something glows, it lights up.

Other fish see the glowing line. They swim to it. They want to see what is glowing. Snap! A mouth bites down. Something is eaten. It is not the anglerfish! It is the fish that comes to look at the light. The anglerfish tricks fish with its light.

An insect is on a branch. Some old bird dropping is on the branch, too, but that is all. The insect thinks it is alone. It thinks it is safe. Snap! A mouth bites down. Something is eaten. It is not the bird dropping! It is the insect that thought it was alone.

The bird dropping is not a bird dropping. It is an insect that looks like a bird dropping. The insect mimics a bird dropping. When you mimic something, you look like it. You copy it. The insect tricks other insects by mimicking a bird dropping.

Animal Tricks

After reading the story, answer the questions.
Fill in the circle next to the correct answer.

1. This story is mainly about

    (a) insects that can mimic

    (b) worms in a turtle's mouth

    (c) how some animals catch food

    (d) how anglerfish use a fishing line

2. Why do fish swim to the anglerfish's "fishing line"?

    (a) the tip glows

    (b) the tip is pink

    (c) the tip wiggles

    (d) the tip looks like a worm

3. One insect looks like a branch. The insect is _____ the branch.

    (a) eating

    (b) glowing

    (c) tricking

    (d) mimicking

4. Think about how the word **down** relates to **up**. Which words relate in the same way?

    down : up

    (a) worm : pink

    (b) light : dark

    (c) ocean : water

    (d) tongue : mouth

5. From the story, you can tell that

    (a) all animals play tricks

    (b) all animals catch food the same way

    (c) not all animals get food the same way

    (d) all animals cannot see in the dark oceans

Out of Air

These are new words to practice.

Say each word 10 times.

* ocean   * signal

* breathe   * mouthpiece

* experiment   * marine

* partner   * biologist

Choose one new word to write.

_____

\- \-

_____

Out of Air

Sylvia Earle was in the ocean. She was under the water. She was swimming. She was looking at a fish. The fish was eating a plant. A tank was on Earle's back. The tank was full of air. Earle was breathing the air in the tank.

Suddenly, Earle could not breathe. She had no air. She needed to breathe. Earle was part of an experiment. She was living under the water. She was living with four other women. They were all living under the water. They were living in a science lab. The science lab was under the water.

Earle swam to her dive partner. She gave a signal. It was the "out of air" signal. Earle moved her finger across her neck. Earle's dive partner knew the signal. Earle's partner took her mouthpiece out of her mouth. She gave it to Earle. Earle took a breath. Then, she gave the mouthpiece back to her partner. The two partners shared air. They swam back to the lab, sharing air.

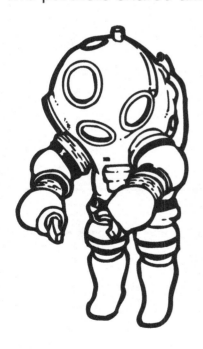

Earle was a marine biologist. A marine biologist studies ocean life. Earle studied ocean life. Earle liked living in the science lab. She lived in the lab for two weeks. One time Earle was part of another experiment. She walked on the ocean floor. She walked alone. She was not tied to anything.

How did Earle walk on the ocean floor? She got in a Jim suit. A Jim suit has arms. It has legs, too. It has a big head. It has windows in the head. Earle got inside the suit. She looked like a big robot. Earle went down 1,250 feet (381 meters)! Earle was the first person to go this deep and walk alone. Earle saw new things. She liked the experiment in the Jim suit.

34

Out of Air

After reading the story, answer the questions.
Fill in the circle next to the correct answer.

1. This story is mainly about
   - (a) a Jim suit.
   - (b) a mouthpiece.
   - (c) a science lab.
   - (d) a marine biologist.

2. What did Earle's dive partner share?
   - (a) air
   - (b) a tank
   - (c) a signal
   - (d) a Jim suit

3. What might a marine biologist study?
   - (a) fish
   - (b) rocks
   - (c) robots
   - (d) the sun

4. Think about how the word **see** relates to **saw**. Which words relate in the same way?

   | **see : saw** |

   - (a) eats : eat
   - (b) swim : swam
   - (c) walk : walks
   - (d) breathe : breathing

5. If you are alone, you do not have a
   - (a) lab
   - (b) tank
   - (c) partner
   - (d) Jim suit

The Month of June— Summer or Winter?

These are new words to practice.

Say each word 10 times.

* June

* summer

* winter

* orbits

* tilts

* length

* temperature

* equator

Choose one new word to write.

_____

- -

_____

36

The Month of June—
Summer or Winter?

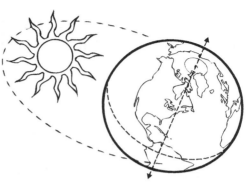

Sam said, "I like June. June is a good month. I like it hot. Summer starts in June. Summer days are hot. The days in June are hot."

Pam said, "I like June. June is a good month. I like it cold. Winter starts in June. Winter days are cold. The days in June are cold." Who is right? Are the days in June hot or cold?

Sam is right. Pam is right. How can both Sam and Pam be right? Our Earth orbits around the Sun. It goes around the Sun. It circles the Sun. As it orbits, it tilts. When something tilts, it leans. For half of Earth's orbit, the North Pole points toward the Sun. For half of Earth's orbit, the South Pole points toward the Sun.

When the North Pole points toward the sun, it is warmer in the north. More of the Sun's light hits the northern part of the Earth. The days are longer. In the south, it is colder. The days are shorter. When the South Pole points toward the Sun, it is warmer in the south. More of the sun's light hits the southern part of the Earth. The days are longer. In the north, it is colder. The days are shorter.

Sam lives in the north. Summer starts in June for Sam. Pam lives in the south. Winter starts in June for Pam. But what about Cam? All of Cam's days are about the same length. They are not long. They are not short. All of Cam's days are about the same temperature. Where does Cam live? Cam lives in the middle. He lives near the equator. Near the equator, it does not matter which way the Earth tilts. The temperature and day length stay about the same.

The Month of June— Summer or Winter?

After reading the story, answer the questions.
Fill in the circle next to the correct answer.

1. This story is mainly about

   (a) Sam, Pam, and Cam
   (b) the North and South Poles
   (c) what the days are like in June
   (d) the temperature at the equator

2. Where does Sam live?

   (a) near the Sun
   (b) in the north
   (c) in the south
   (d) near the equator

3. Think about how the word **hot** relates to **cold**. Which words relate in the same way?

hot : cold

   (a) lean : tilt
   (b) long : short
   (c) equator : middle
   (d) temperature : length

4. When the South Pole points toward the sun,

   (a) the days are colder in the south
   (b) the days are warmer in the north
   (c) the days are longer in the north
   (d) the days are longer in the south

5. When something orbits, it

   (a) points to
   (b) tilts or leans
   (c) is in the middle
   (d) goes around or circles

Leaf Detective

These are new words to practice.

Say each word 10 times.

✳ floor	✳ jungle
✳ shady	✳ smooth
✳ leaves	✳ covered
✳ detective	✳ spines

Choose one new word to write.

_____

- - - - - - - - - - - - - - - - -

_____

Leaf Detective

You are on a forest floor. It is dark. It is cool. It is shady. The big, high trees shade you. They keep the sun from burning you. They keep the forest cool. You look at the plants close to you. You look at the plants, low on the forest floor. Think about the leaves on the low plants. Think like a detective. Do you think the leaves will be big or little?

Plants need sun. They need sunlight to grow. They need sunlight to make food. Plants on the forest floor have big leaves. The leaves are very large. The big leaves let the plant make the best use of any light that reaches them. The big, high trees block the sunlight. They make the forest dark and shady. Still, the plants on the forest floor can live. They can get enough sunlight with their big, large leaves.

One plant lives in the water. The plant is a water lily. It lives in jungles. Each water lily has 40 to 50 leaves. The leaves float on top of the water. They are very large. Each leaf is about six feet (1.8 meters) across! The leaves are strong. A child can walk across them! Think about the jungle water lily leaves. Think like a detective. How does a water lily keep fish from eating its leaves?

Some leaves feel smooth. Leaves of the giant water lily are not smooth. The bottoms of the leaves are covered. They are covered in spines. The spines are sharp. The sharp spines keep fish from eating the leaves.

Some trees have leaves that taste bad. Think like a detective. Why do some plants have bad-tasting leaves? If a leaf tastes bad, they will not be eaten. Insects and animals do not like bad-tasting leaves.

Leaf Detective

After reading the story, answer the questions.
Fill in the circle next to the correct answer.

1. What keeps a fish from eating a jungle water lily?

   (a) big leaves

   (b) smooth leaves

   (c) leaves with spines

   (d) leaves that taste bad

2. This story is mainly about

   (a) leaves

   (b) detectives

   (c) the water lily

   (d) the forest floor

3. What do plants need?

   (a) shade

   (b) spines

   (c) leaves

   (d) sunlight

4. The leaves at the top of big, high forest trees are most likely

   (a) bad-tasting

   (b) covered in spines

   (c) bigger than the leaves on the low forest plants

   (d) smaller than the leaves on the low forest plants

5. Think about how the word **bad** relates to **good**. Which words relate in the same way?

bad : good

   (a) low : high

   (b) big : large

   (c) forest : floor

   (d) smooth : spines

Spiders

These are new words to practice.

Say each word 10 times.

∗ spider	∗ sticky
∗ protect	∗ crawling
∗ insects	∗ orb
∗ silk	∗ weavers

Choose one new word to write.

_____

- - - - - - - - - - - - - - - - -

_____

Spiders

A spider has eight legs. It has eight eyes. Most spiders help us. Only a few spiders can hurt us. Many spiders protect plants. How do spiders protect plants? Spiders eat insects. They eat insects that eat plants.

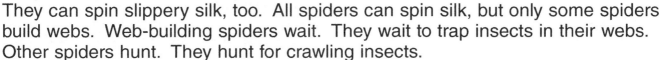

Spiders can spin silk. They can spin fat silk. They can spin thin silk. They can spin sticky silk. They can spin slippery silk, too. All spiders can spin silk, but only some spiders build webs. Web-building spiders wait. They wait to trap insects in their webs. Other spiders hunt. They hunt for crawling insects.

Some spiders are orb weavers. Orb weavers build webs shaped like an orb. An orb is like a circle. When an insect hits the web, the spider feels the web vibrating. When something is vibrating, it is moving back and forth. The spider rushes to the insect. It wraps it up. It wraps it up with sticky silk. Then, it bites it. This way the spider does not get hurt. This way the spider can wait to eat.

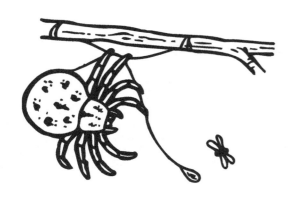

One spider is a "net-thrower." The spider makes a net with its silk. Then it hangs upside down. It holds its net. It waits for an insect to crawl by. When an insect crawls by, the spider throws its net. It throws its net over the crawling insect!

One spider spins a ball of sticky silk. It fastens the sticky ball to a line. The line is made of strong silk. Then, the spider tricks male moths. The spider makes the smell of the female moth. Male moths come to find the female moth. When a male moth comes, the spider hits it with the sticky ball of silk! The moth gets stuck. The spider then pulls in its line. The spider gets the stuck moth!

Spiders

**After reading the story, answer the questions.
Fill in the circle next to the correct answer.**

1. What does an orb weaver's web look like?

   ⓐ a net

   ⓑ a ball

   ⓒ a line

   ⓓ a circle

2. When something is vibrating, it

   ⓐ protects plants

   ⓑ hangs upside down

   ⓒ moves back and forth

   ⓓ smells like a female moth

3. This story is mainly about

   ⓐ webs

   ⓑ silk

   ⓒ insects

   ⓓ spiders

4. Which statement is true?

   ⓐ All spiders can spin silk.

   ⓑ All spiders can build webs.

   ⓒ Some spiders have eight legs.

   ⓓ Some spiders have eight eyes.

5. Think about how the word **boy** relates to **girl**. Which words relate in the same way?

boy : girl

   ⓐ web : net

   ⓑ male : female

   ⓒ insect : spider

   ⓓ plant : protect

Harder Than Bone

These are new words to practice.

Say each word 10 times.

✻ skeleton	✻ canines
✻ teeth	✻ pierce
✻ enamel	✻ molars
✻ incisors	✻ grind

Choose one new word to write.

_____

- -

_____

Harder than Bone

You have bones. Bones make up your skeleton. Your bones are hard. Your skeleton holds up your body. You have something else in your body. It covers something. It is harder than bone. What could it be?

You have teeth. Teeth are in your mouth. You use your teeth. You use your teeth to break down food. You break down food into small pieces. Teeth have enamel. Enamel is on the outside of the tooth. Enamel covers the tooth. Enamel is hard. It is harder than bone. It is the hardest thing in your body.

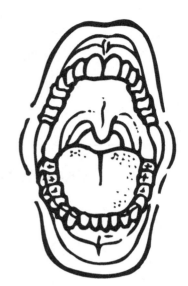

Your teeth have different shapes. Why do teeth have different shapes? Different teeth have different jobs. Some teeth are incisors. Incisors are flat. They are sharp. They are in front of your mouth. You use them to slice. Incisors can slice like a knife. You have eight incisors. Four incisors are in your upper jaw. Four incisors are in your lower jaw.

You have four canine teeth. Canines are sharp. They are next to your incisors. You use your canines to pierce food. When you pierce something, you pass into it. You put a hole in it. Your canines grip your food while you tear off a bite. You have molars. Molars are large. Molars are flat. They are behind the canines. Molars grind up food. When you grind something, you crush it into tiny bits.

We eat different foods. We eat plants. We eat meat. We need all our teeth. We use different teeth with different foods. A lion eats meat. It has big canines to help it bite and tear meat. A horse eats grass. It does not eat meat. A horse has big, flat molars. It needs the molars to grind up grass. It does not need big canines.

46

Harder Than Bone

After reading the story, answer the questions.
Fill in the circle next to the correct answer.

1. This story is mainly about

   ⓐ food

   ⓑ teeth

   ⓒ bones

   ⓓ enamel

2. A flat tooth that slices like a knife is

   ⓐ a molar

   ⓑ a canine

   ⓒ an incisor

   ⓓ in the back of your mouth

3. When you eat rice, you _____ the rice with your molars.

   ⓐ grip

   ⓑ grind

   ⓒ slice

   ⓓ pierce

4. Think about how the word **tooth** relates to **teeth**. Which words relate in the same way?

   | tooth : teeth |

   ⓐ foot : feet

   ⓑ lion : lions

   ⓒ horse : horses

   ⓓ incisors : incisor

5. If an animal has very big, sharp canines, it is likely that the animal eats

   ⓐ meat

   ⓑ grass

   ⓒ bones

   ⓓ enamel

Glacier: Ice on the Move

These are new words to practice.
Say each word 10 times.

✳ mountain	✳ spread
✳ extinct	✳ sheet
✳ glacier	✳ valley
✳ bottom	✳ flow

Choose one new word to write.

_____

- -

_____

Glacier: Ice on the Move

A man was walking. It was 1933. He saw a sheep. The man looked again. Could he believe his eyes? Yes, it was a sheep. It was a mountain sheep. It was a kind of sheep that was not alive anymore! It was extinct. When something is extinct, it is no longer alive.

The mountain sheep did not move. The man went close. Still, the sheep did not move. The man went closer. He touched the sheep. The sheep was not alive. It was frozen. Long ago, the sheep had fallen into a crack. The crack was in a glacier. Over time, the glacier had moved. Over time, ice at the glacier's end had melted. After many years, the sheep was free of ice.

What is a glacier? A glacier is snow and ice. It snows. Fresh snow falls on the old snow. More and more snow falls. Every year, more snow falls. The pile of snow gets big. All the snow is heavy. It presses on the old bottom snow. The snow on the bottom melts. It turns to ice.

The ice at the bottom begins to move. It spreads out. It goes downhill. When the snow pile begins to move, it is called a glacier. The glacier moves at different speeds. The bottom moves faster. The bottom ice moves faster. It moves faster than the snow and ice at the top. The glacier cracks. It cracks as its top and bottom move at different speeds.

Glaciers that spread out are called ice sheets. The ice sheet near the South Pole is thick. It is more than 2 miles (3 kilometers) thick! Glaciers that go downhill are called valley glaciers. They flow between mountains. Most valley glaciers flow about 650 feet (200 meters) a year.

Glacier: Ice on the Move

After reading the story, answer the questions.
Fill in the circle next to the correct answer.

1. A glacier that flows between mountains is called

   ⓐ a crack
   ⓑ an ice sheet
   ⓒ a fresh glacier
   ⓓ a valley glacier

2. Why do cracks form in glaciers?

   ⓐ ice at the glacier's end melts
   ⓑ fresh snow presses on the old bottom snow
   ⓒ bottom ice flows faster than top snow and ice
   ⓓ top snow and ice flows faster than bottom ice

3. This story is mainly about

   ⓐ glaciers
   ⓑ ice sheets
   ⓒ snow and ice
   ⓓ a frozen sheep

4. When something is extinct,

   ⓐ it is frozen
   ⓑ it is a sheep
   ⓒ it flows downhill
   ⓓ it is no longer alive

5. Think about how the word **fresh** relates to **old**. Which words relate in the same way?

fresh : old

   ⓐ speed : move
   ⓑ ice : spread
   ⓒ top : bottom
   ⓓ glacier : snow

Paper

These are new words to practice.

Say each word 10 times.

✳ words	✳ reeds
✳ paper	✳ mixture
✳ tablets	✳ mush
✳ heavy	✳ captured

Choose one new word to write.

_____

- -

_____

Paper

You are reading words. What are the words on? The words are on paper. Books are made of paper. Newspapers are paper. You can write and draw on paper. You can wrap things and make kites with paper. You use paper a lot. You use it every day!

Long ago, people did not have paper. They made clay tablets. They scratched letters in the tablets. The tablets were big. They were heavy. They took a long time to make. Around 3000 B.C., people in Egypt made something new. They made a type of paper. It was made of reeds. Reeds are a kind of plant. It was better than tablets. Still, it took a long time to make.

The first true paper was made in China. It was made in the year 105. A man mixed things. He mixed tree bark, fishnets, and bamboo. He put them in a pot. He added water. He hit the mixture. He hit it with a stick. The stick was big and heavy. The man hit the mixture again and again. The mixture turned into mush. The man took the mush. He spread it over a screen. He let it dry. He had made the first true paper!

No one else knew how to make paper. Then, in the year 751, some men were captured. The men were from China. They knew how to make paper. The men were brought to a new city. The captured men taught other people how to make paper. Soon, people all over the world learned how to make paper.

What did paper do for science? Paper did a lot for science. Paper is light. It is easy to move. People could write down what they knew on paper. They could share what they knew with people far away.

Paper

After reading the story, answer the questions.
Fill in the circle next to the correct answer.

1. What did people use in Egypt to make paper?

   ⓐ clay
   ⓑ reeds
   ⓒ bamboo
   ⓓ fishnets

2. This story is mainly about

   ⓐ China
   ⓑ paper
   ⓒ tablets
   ⓓ science

3. Why is paper better than tablets?

   ⓐ Paper is a mixture.
   ⓑ Paper has words on it.
   ⓒ Paper is light and easy to move.
   ⓓ Paper is made all over the world.

4. Which answer is in the correct order? The first true paper was made by

   ⓐ letting the mush dry, putting things in a pot, hitting the mixture
   ⓑ hitting the mixture, putting things in a pot, spreading mush over a screen
   ⓒ putting things in a pot, letting the mush dry, spreading mush over a screen
   ⓓ putting things in a pot, hitting the mixture, spreading mush over a screen

5. Think about how the word **light** relates to **heavy**. Which words relate in the same way?

   | **light : heavy** |

   ⓐ easy : hard
   ⓑ spread : dry
   ⓒ tablets : clay
   ⓓ captured : knew

Creature in the Dark

These are new words to practice.

Say each word 10 times.

* newt   * creatures

* blind   * important

* cave   * life

* protects   * streams

Choose one new word to write.

_____

- - - - - - - - - - - - - - - - - -

_____

Creature in the Dark

Di saw a newt. The newt was small. The newt was blind. It could not see. The newt was pale. It had thin skin. Di looked at the newt. She said, "I know where this newt lives. I know by its pale, thin skin. I know by its size. I know because it is blind."

Di said, "This newt lives in a cave. Sunlight cannot go into a cave. It is dark. Skin protects us from the burning sun. Skin keeps us from drying out. Creatures in caves do not need thick skin. Their skin is damp. It does not dry out. Their skin does not need to protect them from burning sun.

"The newt is blind. Most cave creatures are blind. It is dark in a cave. What good are eyes? Eyes are not important in a cave. The newt is pale. Its skin has no color. Skin color is not important in a dark cave. There is no light to see color by. Colored skin does not help you hide in a cave."

Di said, "The newt is small. A big creature needs lots of food. There is not a lot of food in a cave. All cave creatures are small." Di said, "Now, I have a question. Plants are important to cave life. But plants need sunlight. Plants cannot grow in a cave. How can plants be important to cave life?"

Caves with life have water. The water comes from streams. The streams are underground. Bits of dead plants and bat droppings are in the water. Bats eat fruits from plants. Bats eat insects that need plants. The dead plants and bat droppings are food. They are food for some cave creatures. They are food for the creatures the newt eats.

Creature in the Dark

After reading the story, answer the questions.
Fill in the circle next to the correct answer.

1. This story is mainly about

   (a) cave newts

   (b) dark caves

   (c) cave creatures

   (d) plants in caves

2. How did Di know the newt lived in a cave?

   (a) It was big.

   (b) It was blind.

   (c) It had small eyes.

   (d) It had colored skin.

3. Can a cave newt live without plants?

   (a) No, the newt eats plants.

   (b) Yes, the newt does not eat plants.

   (c) No, the newt eats creatures that eat plants.

   (d) Yes, plants need sunlight, and a cave is dark.

4. Think about how the word **big** relates to **small**. Which words relate in the same way?

   > **big : small**

   (a) dark : light

   (b) pale : color

   (c) water : stream

   (d) plant : sunlight

5. Which is not a creature?

   (a) bat

   (b) newt

   (c) light

   (d) insect

The Way the Wind Blows

These are new words to practice.

Say each word 10 times.

* quietly   * points

* observation   * windsock

* weather   * Arctic

* vane   * desert

Choose one new word to write.

_____

- -

_____

The Way the Wind Blows

A man is quiet. He picks up dust or leaves. Quietly, he throws the dust or leaves into the air. He watches what way they go. Why does the man quietly throw the dust or leaves? Why does he throw them into the air? Why does he watch what way they go? The man is making an observation. He is seeing what way the wind is blowing.

Why does the man want to know what way the wind is blowing? The man is a hunter. He does not want animals to smell him. He wants to be downwind of the animals. He does not want the wind to blow his smell to the animals. The man uses the dust or leaves as a tool. He uses them to see what way the wind is blowing.

Scientists think measuring the way the wind blew was one of the first weather observations man ever made. A weather vane is a tool. A weather vane turns. It points. It turns and points the way the wind is blowing. Weather vanes were first made long ago. We still use weather vanes today.

A windsock is a tool, too. A windsock is like a long sock. It is on a pole. It is open at both ends. The wind fills it up. The wind blows through it. We can look at the sock. We can see what way the wind is blowing.

We use tools to make weather observations. We learn from our observations. We learn what way winds often blow when they bring cold air. We learn what way winds often blow when they bring warm air. Some winds come from the cold Arctic. These Arctic winds bring cold air. Some winds come from the hot desert. These desert winds bring warm air.

The Way the Wind Blows

After reading the story, answer the questions.
Fill in the circle next to the correct answer.

1. How were the first weather observations made?

   (a) by throwing up dust and leaves

   (b) by hanging windsocks on a pole

   (c) by learning what way winds blow hot and cold air

   (d) by seeing what way a weather vane turns and points

2. This story is mainly about

   (a) tools

   (b) hunters long ago

   (c) cold and hot winds

   (d) weather observations

3. If someone makes an observation, he is

   (a) seeing how something is

   (b) looking for dust and leaves

   (c) learning what way the wind blows

   (d) downwind of animals so the animals cannot smell him

4. Which winds often bring cold air?

   (a) winds that blow to the desert

   (b) winds that blow to the Arctic

   (c) winds that blow from the desert

   (d) winds that blow from the Arctic

5. Think about how the word **hot** relates to **cold**. Which words relate in the same way?

hot : cold

   (a) wind : blows

   (b) quiet : noise

   (c) turn : around

   (d) windsock : pole

Tools in the Wild

These are new words to practice.

Say each word 10 times.

* binoculars   * stems

* chimpanzee   * twigs

* attention   * termites

* ignored   * mound

Choose one new word to write.

_____

- -

_____

Tools in the Wild

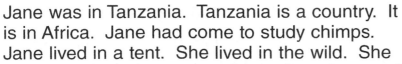

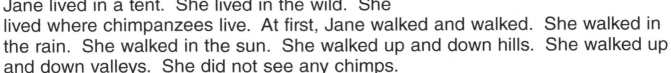

Jane was tired. She was wet. She had walked up and down three valleys. Then, she saw something. She saw something move. Jane picked up her binoculars. She looked through her binoculars. She saw a chimpanzee. She sat still. She looked for a long time. She wanted to see what the chimp was doing.

Jane was in Tanzania. Tanzania is a country. It is in Africa. Jane had come to study chimps. Jane lived in a tent. She lived in the wild. She lived where chimpanzees live. At first, Jane walked and walked. She walked in the rain. She walked in the sun. She walked up and down hills. She walked up and down valleys. She did not see any chimps.

At last Jane saw chimpanzees. It took many months. At first the chimps ran away from Jane. Over time, they got used to her. Over time, the chimps did not pay attention to Jane. They ignored her. When you ignore something, you do not pay attention to it. The chimps ignored Jane. The chimps acted as if Jane was not there.

So what was the chimp doing? The chimp was making tools! No one had ever seen chimps make tools before! How was the chimp making tools? The chimp took small stems and twigs. It was tearing leaves off of the stems and twigs. It was bending the stems and twigs.

What were the tools for? The tools were for termites! Termites are insects. They live in big mounds. First, the chimp scratched the mound. It made a small opening. Then, the chimp stuck in its twig. When the chimp pulled the twig out, termites were on it! Quickly, the chimp ate the termites. By watching, Jane learned that big chimps teach small chimps how to make these tools.

Tools in the Wild

After reading the story, answer the questions.
Fill in the circle next to the correct answer.

1. Why was Jane living in the wild?

   (a) She wanted to live in a tent.

   (b) She wanted to learn about chimpanzees.

   (c) She wanted to learn how to make tools.

   (d) She wanted chimps to pay attention to her.

2. This story is mainly about

   (a) Jane and tools

   (b) tools and termites

   (c) Jane and chimpanzees

   (d) Tanzania and chimpanzees

3. Binoculars are

   (a) a tent

   (b) a tool

   (c) a mound

   (d) a country

4. Which statement is true?

   (a) Termites use tools.

   (b) Tanzania is an insect.

   (c) Jane ignored the chimpanzees.

   (d) It took Jane a long time to see chimpanzees.

5. Think about how the word **up** relates to **down**. Which words relate in the same way?

up : down

   (a) live : tent

   (b) ignore : in

   (c) watch : learn

   (d) hill : valley

Dry Deserts

These are new words to practice.

Say each word 10 times.

* desert   * temperature

* dry   * protect

* water   * swell

* ground   * shrink

Choose one new word to write.

Dry Deserts

Think of a desert. Did you think of a dry place? A desert is a dry place. There is little water in a desert. It does not rain often. There are only a few plants in a desert. This is because there is not much water. In some deserts, it rains less than one inch (2.54 centimeters) a year!

Did you think of a hot place? Most deserts are hot. How hot is hot? Ground temperatures can get to 180°F (83°C)! You do not need a stove! You can fry an egg on the ground! Think about walking. You would need shoes. You would need shoes to protect your feet. You would need to protect your feet from the hot ground.

What about air temperature? Air temperature can be very hot. Air temperature was taken in one desert. The desert was in North Africa. The temperature was taken in the shade. It was 136°F (58°C)! Think about your clothes. You would have to protect your skin. You would have to protect your skin with clothes.

Some deserts are cold. They are cold at night. The temperature drops. It drops to below freezing. Lots of deserts are sand deserts. Why do so many deserts have sand? Heat makes rock swell. Cold makes rocks shrink. When rocks swell and shrink, they break up. They turn into sand.

The fennec is a fox. It is the world's smallest fox. Fennecs live in deserts in North Africa. How does the fennec stay cool in the hot desert? The fennec sleeps in the day. It sleeps when it is hot. It hunts at night. It hunts when it is cool. The fennec has very big ears. Body heat goes out the ears. Big ears help the fox stay cool.

Dry Deserts

**After reading the story, answer the questions.
Fill in the circle next to the correct answer.**

1. What does heat do to rocks?

   (a) It makes them swell.

   (b) It makes them shrink.

   (c) It makes the break up.

   (d) It makes them turn into sand.

2. Why might you need good shoes in a desert?

   (a) so you can let out body heat

   (b) so you can protect your skin in the shade

   (c) so you do not burn your feet on the hot ground

   (d) so you can stay warm when it gets cool at night

3. This story is mainly about

   (a) fennecs

   (b) deserts

   (c) North Africa

   (d) air and ground temperature

4. Which statement is most likely true?

   (a) All foxes have big ears.

   (b) Foxes in cold places have smaller ears than desert foxes.

   (c) Foxes in cold places have much bigger ears than desert foxes.

   (d) Foxes in cold places can hear better than foxes in hot places.

5. Think about how the word **heat** relates to **cool**. Which words relate in the same way?

heat : cool

   (a) burn : fry

   (b) water : rain

   (c) fennec : fox

   (d) swell : shrink

Light and Dark

These are new words to practice.

Say each word 10 times.

✳ penguin	✳ below
✳ lapwing	✳ protect
✳ colors	✳ disguise
✳ above	✳ sneak

Choose one new word to write.

_____

- -

_____

Light and Dark

A penguin is a bird. A lapwing is a bird. A shark is a fish. The penguin, lapwing, and shark are the same in one way. How can birds be like a fish? How can a penguin, lapwing, and shark be the same in one way?

A penguin is two colors. It is black and white. The black is on the top. A penguin's back is black. It is dark above. The white is on the bottom. A penguin's belly is white. It is light below. Why is a penguin dark and light? A penguin's colors help keep it safe. Its colors help protect it.

Penguins swim a lot. Animals swimming below the penguin have a hard time seeing it. This is because the white color looks like the lighter top water. Animals swimming above the penguin have a hard time seeing it. This is because the black color looks like the dark deep water.

Lapwings are dark and light. They are dark green and white. The green is on the top. A lapwing's back is green. A lapwing's belly is white. Lapwings stand in green grass. They cannot be seen from above. They are green like the grass. When a lapwing flies, it is hidden from animals below. It's white belly are hard to see in the light sky. The lapwing's colors help protect it.

Sharks are dark and light, too. They are dark on top. They are light on the bottom. The dark and light coloring makes the shark hard to see. It helps disguise its shape. It helps hide its shape. A shark can sneak up on fish. It can sneak up on fish from above or below. Fish have a hard seeing the shark in its light-and-dark disguise.

Light and Dark

**After reading the story, answer the questions.
Fill in the circle next to the correct answer.**

1. This story is mainly about

   ⓐ light and dark

   ⓑ penguins and lapwings

   ⓒ the colors of some animals

   ⓓ how some animals sneak up on others

2. How are the birds and the shark the same?

   ⓐ They all are animals that are black.

   ⓑ They are all dark above and light below.

   ⓒ They all are animals that live in water.

   ⓓ They are all light above and dark below.

3. Think about how the word **top** relates to **above**. Which words relate in the same way?

top : above

   ⓐ dark : light

   ⓑ color : black

   ⓒ bottom : below

   ⓓ penguin : bird

4. When something is disguised, it is

   ⓐ safe

   ⓑ hidden

   ⓒ swimming

   ⓓ protected

5. Why do lapwings need dark green backs?

   ⓐ to sneak up on fish

   ⓑ to fly in the light sky

   ⓒ to swim in dark deep water

   ⓓ to be hidden when they stand in dark green grass

Shoots Up, Roots Down

These are new words to practice.

Say each word 10 times.

✳ nutrients	✳ potato
✳ tube	✳ South America
✳ gravity	✳ Andes Mountains
✳ respond	✳ thaw

Choose one new word to write.

_____

- -

_____

Shoots Up, Roots Down

A root is part of a plant. Roots grow down. They go down into the soil. Roots hold a plant in the soil. Plants suck up water through their roots. They suck up nutrients, too. Plants need water to grow. They need water to stay healthy. Plants need nutrients. Nutrients are in food. Plants need nutrients to stay healthy.

Roots are really just tubes. What does a tube look like? A straw is a tube. You can sip water through a tube. Roots are tubes pushed into the soil. Smaller tubes grow out of bigger tubes. Even smaller tubes grow out of the smaller tubes. The smallest tubes are called root hairs. Only water and nutrients can pass through the walls of the root hairs.

How do roots know to grow down? How do shoots know to grow up? Gravity is a force. The force pulls things toward the center of the Earth. The roots respond to gravity. The shoots respond to gravity. The roots grow down. The shoots grow up. The shoots grow up to the light.

We eat roots. We eat carrots and potatoes. A potato is a tuber. A tuber is a special part of the root. The first potatoes came from South America. They were grown in the Andes Mountains. Explorers brought potatoes from South America to Europe. Today, potatoes are eaten all over the world.

People high in the Andes Mountains keep their potatoes from rotting. How do they do this? They freeze-dry their potatoes. They let the potatoes freeze at night. They thaw them in the day. They let the sun warm them. Over and over they freeze and thaw the potatoes. The potatoes dry out. No water is left in the potatoes. The dried-out potatoes do not rot.

Shoots Up, Roots Down

After reading the story, answer the questions.
Fill in the circle next to the correct answer.

1. This story is mainly about

   ⓐ tubes

   ⓑ roots

   ⓒ gravity

   ⓓ potatoes

2. When something is freeze-dried,

   ⓐ it is a potato

   ⓑ it is a root hair

   ⓒ it has no water in it

   ⓓ it responds to gravity

3. Think about how the word **up** relates to **down**. Which words relate in the same way?

up : down

   ⓐ light : day

   ⓑ freeze : dry

   ⓒ shoot : root

   ⓓ high : mountains

4. The smallest roots are called

   ⓐ tubes

   ⓑ carrots

   ⓒ nutrients

   ⓓ root hairs

5. What makes roots grow down?

   ⓐ light

   ⓑ water

   ⓒ tubers

   ⓓ gravity

Why Bruises Change Color

These are new words to practice.

Say each word 10 times.

* bruise   * capillaries

* blood   * cells

* tubes   * building

* vessels   * absorbs

Choose one new word to write.

_____

\- -

_____

Why Bruises Change Color

You bump your arm. You bump it hard. You do not get cut. Your skin does not break. Still, you get a bruise. Your skin turns blue-black. What is a bruise? Why does your skin turn blue-black?

Blood flows in your body. Blood flows through tubes. Tubes that carry blood are called blood vessels. How many miles of blood vessels do you have? You have about 60,000 miles (96,000 kilometers) of blood vessels! You have enough blood vessels to go around the world! Some tubes are big. Some tubes are tiny. The tiny tubes are called capillaries.

Living things are made of cells. Cells are like building blocks. They are the smallest building block of living things. Your body has lots of cells. It has many kinds of cells. You have bone cells. You have skin cells. You have blood cells, too. You have lots of blood cells. Most of your blood cells are red blood cells. Red blood cells make your blood look red.

When you get bumped, you may not get cut. Still, you may hurt some capillaries. Some may break. Blood leaks from the capillaries. You bleed under your skin. When blood cells leak from the capillaries, they die. When the cells die, they turn blue-black. We see the blue-black color. We call the blue-black color a bruise.

Your body absorbs the dead blood cells. When something is absorbed, it is taken in. It is made part of itself. Fresh blood absorbs the dead blood cells. It takes many days. The bruise changes color. It changes color as the fresh blood absorbs the dead cells. It changes from blue-black to purple. It changes from purple to yellow. Finally, the bruise is gone. All the dead blood cells have been absorbed.

Why Bruises Change Color

After reading the story, answer the questions.
Fill in the circle next to the correct answer.

1. What are living things made of?

   (a) blood

   (b) cells

   (c) vessels

   (d) capillaries

2. This story is mainly about

   (a) cells

   (b) blood

   (c) bruises

   (d) capillaries

3. If your bruise is yellow, it means that

   (a) your capillaries are leaking

   (b) you are bleeding under the skin

   (c) soon the bruise will change to blue-black

   (d) most of the dead blood cells have been absorbed

4. Which statement is true?

   (a) Vessels and capillaries are cells.

   (b) You do not have many blood vessels.

   (c) When you get a bruise, you cut your skin.

   (d) Red blood cells make your blood look red.

5. Think about how the word **tiny** relates to **small**. Which words relate in the same way?

tiny : small

   (a) many : lots

   (b) blood : red

   (c) bump : bruise

   (d) yellow : color

An Old Made New

These are new words to practice.

Say each word 10 times.

✳ strong	✳ lesson
✳ shined	✳ solid
✳ brightly	✳ melted
✳ change	✳ liquid

Choose one new word to write.

_____

- -

_____

An Old Made New

Sun said he was strong. Wind said he was stronger than Sun. Sun and Wind saw a man. The man had on a coat. Sun said, "We shall see who is stronger. We shall see who is strong enough to make the man take off his coat."

Wind blew. He blew and blew. The man bent over. It was hard for him to stand. Still, he did not take off his coat. The more the wind blew, the tighter the man held his coat. Sun said, "Now, it is my turn. I can make the man take off his coat. You will see." Sun shined brightly. Sun's bright light made it hot. The man got hot. The man got so hot that he took off his coat.

This story about who is stronger is an old story. We could change it for today. We could change it to a lesson about solids. A solid takes up space. A solid has its own shape. You can make a pile out of solids. A candy bar is a solid.

A man had a candy bar. Sun said, "We shall see who is strong enough to make the man give up his candy bar." Wind blew and blew. The man held on to his candy bar. The more the wind blew, the tighter the man held on. Sun said, "Now, it is my turn." Sun shined brightly. Sun's bright light made it hot. The candy bar got so hot that it melted. It turned into a liquid. The man did not want a melted candy bar. He threw it away.

What is today's lesson? Today's lesson is that heat can turn solids into liquids. Wind cannot turn solids into liquids. Solids will melt if they are heated up.

An Old Made New

**After reading the story, answer the questions.
Fill in the circle next to the correct answer.**

1. When something melts, it becomes

   a) a solid
   b) stronger
   c) a liquid
   d) brighter

2. Why did the man take off his coat?

   a) It melted.
   b) He was hot.
   c) The wind blew and blew.
   d) He wanted to show the sun was stronger.

3. This story is mainly about

   a) what is a solid
   b) an old story with a new lesson
   c) what the sun can do to candy bar
   d) how the wind is stronger than the sun

4. A solid takes up space and has its own shape. You can make a pile out of solids. What is not a solid?

   a) can
   b) rock
   c) milk
   d) banana

5. Think about how the word **wind** relates to **blew**. Which words relate in the same way?

   | **wind : blew** |

   a) coat : hot
   b) bar : candy
   c) story : new
   d) sun : shined

Something Wrong

These are new words to practice.

Say each word 10 times.

* museum   * octopus

* aquarium   * suckers

* camera   * flexible

* pictures   * easily

Choose one new word to write.

_____

- -

_____

Something Wrong

We go to museums. We go to look. We look at things. An aquarium is a museum. It is a museum with fish. Aquariums have lots of tanks. The tanks are filled with fish. The fish come from all over. One big aquarium had lots of tanks. It had lots of fish. The fish were from all over. But something was wrong. Something was wrong in the aquarium.

In the day, nothing was wrong. All the fish were fine. The aquarium closed at night.   No one was there. No one could get in. In the morning, it was not fine. Fish were missing. Something was going on at night. Something wrong was going on. People in the aquarium set up a camera. The camera would take pictures. It would take pictures at night. The pictures would show what was going on.

What was wrong? What did the pictures show? They showed an octopus! They showed an octopus climbing. It was climbing out of its tank. It was going into other tanks. It was eating fish in other tanks. When it was full, it would go back. It would go back to its own tank. In the morning, the octopus was always in its own tank.

How was the octopus climbing? How was it getting out of its tank? It was using its arms. An octopus has eight arms. The arms have suckers. The suckers are round. The suckers are used to grab things. They are used to taste things. They are used to feel things.

The arms are flexible. When something is flexible, it can bend. It can move easily. Why are octopus arms so flexible? Why do they bend so easily? They have no bones. In fact, an octopus does not have any bones at all!

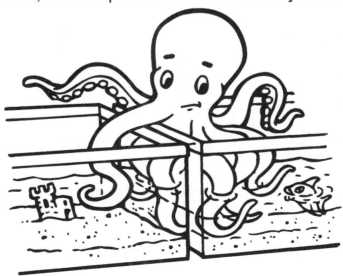

Something Wrong

After reading the story, answer the questions.
Fill in the circle next to the correct answer.

1. This story is mainly about

   ⓐ a museum and what you see

   ⓑ suckers and what they can do

   ⓒ an aquarium and what was in it

   ⓓ an octopus and what it was doing

2. Why did people in the museum set up a camera?

   ⓐ They wanted to look at pictures.

   ⓑ They wanted to see what was going on at night.

   ⓒ They wanted to see an octopus with eight arms.

   ⓓ They wanted to see what was going on in the day.

3. When something is flexible,

   ⓐ it can climb

   ⓑ it is in a museum

   ⓒ it has eight arms

   ⓓ it can bend easily

4. Think about how the word **fish** relates to **aquarium**. Which words relate in the same way?

   > **fish : aquarium**

   ⓐ house : tank

   ⓑ slide : park

   ⓒ animals : zoo

   ⓓ museum : look

5. What does an octopus uses its suckers on its arms for?

   ⓐ to bend, grab, and feel

   ⓑ to eat, grab, and taste

   ⓒ to grab, taste, and feel

   ⓓ to climb, eat, and taste

How Men Were Saved

These are new words to practice.

Say each word 10 times.

* accident   * firefighters

* tunnel   * police

* explosion   * poisonous

* trapped   * inventor

Choose one new word to write.

_____

- -

_____

How Men Were Saved

An accident happened. It was a bad accident. It was in 1916. It was on July 24th. It was in a tunnel. The tunnel was under Lake Erie. Men were working in the tunnel. They were 250 feet (76 meters) below the lake. An explosion happened. Something blew up.

Men were trapped. They were trapped in the tunnel. They could not get out. Firefighters came. Police came. No one could help the men in the tunnel. If they helped the men in the tunnel, they would die. Why would the firefighters die? Why would the police die?

The explosion filled the tunnel with smoke. It filled it with dust. The explosion filled it with gas. The gas was poisonous. A gas is not a solid. A solid takes up space. A solid has its own shape. A gas is not a liquid. A liquid takes the shape of its container. A gas can change shape and size. Our air is made of gases. The poisonous gases in the tunnel spread. They spread out in the tunnel. The poisonous gas made it so no one could help.

Two men came. The two men were brothers. They went into the tunnel. They did not breathe in the smoke. They did not breathe in the dust. They did not breathe in the poisonous gas. They saved 32 men.

How did the two men do it? One of the men was named Morgan. Morgan was born in 1877. His mother had been a slave. Morgan was very smart. He was an inventor. An inventor makes new things. Morgan invented the gas mask. Morgan and his brother wore Morgan's gas masks. They wore gas masks to save the men.

How Men Were Saved

After reading the story, answer the questions.
Fill in the circle next to the correct answer.

1. This story is mainly about

   (a) an explosion

   (b) firefighters and police

   (c) a tunnel under Lake Erie

   (d) a time when Morgan used his gas mask

2. An explosion is when

   (a) men get trapped

   (b) something blows up

   (c) poisonous gas spreads

   (d) a new thing is invented

3. What is true of a gas?

   (a) It has its own shape.

   (b) It is a solid or a liquid.

   (c) It can change shape and size.

   (d) It takes the shape of its container.

4. Think about how the word **see** relates to **eye**. Which words relate in the same way?

   | **see : eye** |

   (a) mask : gas

   (b) tunnel : under

   (c) breathe : nose

   (d) save : trapped

5. How many men did Morgan and his brother save?

   (a) 24

   (b) 32

   (c) 1877

   (d) 1916

Solid, Liquid, or Gas?

These are new words to practice.

Say each word 10 times.

* solid   * sugar

* liquid   * pieces

* gas   * container

* grain   * breathe

Choose one new word to write.

_____

- -

_____

Solid, Liquid, or Gas?

Everything is a solid, a liquid, or a gas. Is a tree a solid? Is a tree a liquid? Is a tree a gas? A tree is a solid. A tree has its own shape. A solid has its own shape. You can feel a tree's shape when you touch it. You can feel a solid's shape when you touch it. A rock is a solid. A book is a solid.

A grain of sugar is very small. A grain of salt is very small. Is sugar a solid? Is salt a solid? Solids can be broken into tiny pieces. The tiny pieces are still solids. Each tiny piece has its own shape. A grain of sugar is a tiny piece. Still, it is a solid. A grain of salt is a tiny piece. Still, it is a solid.

You can make a pile of sugar. You can make a pile of salt. You cannot make a pile with a liquid. A liquid is like water. You cannot make a pile of water. A liquid always takes the shape of its container.

Water always takes the shape of its container. Water can take the shape of a tall, thin glass. Water can take the shape of a short, fat glass. Water cannot make its own shape. A liquid can be thick. A liquid can be thin. Everything you drink is a liquid.

A gas can change its shape. A gas can change its size. A gas spreads out. It spreads out to fill the space it is in. The air around us is a mixture of gases. One gas in air is oxygen. We need oxygen to live. We cannot breathe in a solid. We cannot breathe in a liquid. We can breathe in a gas!

Solid, Liquid, or Gas?

**After reading the story, answer the questions.
Fill in the circle next to the correct answer.**

1. It can change its shape. It can change its size. It can spread out to fill the space it is in. What is it?

   (a) a gas

   (b) a tree

   (c) a solid

   (d) a liquid

2. You can drink milk. What is milk?

   (a) a gas

   (b) a solid

   (c) a liquid

   (d) a container

3. This story is mainly about

   (a) what we breathe

   (b) what something is

   (c) how a tree has a shape

   (d) grains of sugar and salt

4. What is true about liquids?

   (a) You can breathe in liquids.

   (b) You can pour a liquid into a pile.

   (c) You can break a liquid into tiny pieces.

   (d) A liquid takes the shape of its container.

5. Think about how the word **water** relates to **liquid**. Which words relate in the same way?

water : liquid

   (a) oxygen : gas

   (b) drink : solid

   (c) book : liquid

   (d) sugar : liquid

How NOT to Get Eaten

These are new words to practice.

Say each word 10 times.

✳ puffer fish	✳ dull
✳ predator	✳ bright
✳ escape	✳ wiggles
✳ lizard	✳ glides

Choose one new word to write.

_____

- - - - - - - - - - - - - - - - - - -

_____

How NOT to Get Eaten

A fish is in the water. The fish is small. It is a puffer fish. A bigger fish sees the small puffer fish. The bigger fish wants to eat the smaller fish. Animals that eat other animals are called predators. How can the puffer fish escape from the predator?

The puffer fish gets big! It takes in water. It swells up. It becomes big and round. It has spines on its body. The spines stick out when the fish is big and round. The fish is so big that a predator cannot swallow it. The puffer fish escapes from the predator.

A predator sees a lizard. The lizard is small. It is a dull color. When something is dull, it is not bright. The predator comes close. It thinks it has found its dinner. Then something happens. Something bright pops out! It is bright blue. The bright blue thing wiggles. It wiggles back and forth.

The predator stops in surprise. What is the blue wiggling thing? Can it be the dull-colored lizard? The bright blue thing is a tongue. It is the lizard's tongue. The lizard wiggles it to surprise the predator. The lizard escapes from the surprised predator.

A frog is in a tree. The frog lives in a forest. It is a gliding frog. It has big feet. The feet are webbed. A snake sees the frog. The snake is a predator. It wants to eat the frog. The frog leaps. The frog spreads out its big, webbed feet. The frog glides. It uses its big, webbed feet to glide. The frog glides 50 feet (15 meters). It glides to another tree. The frog escapes from the snake.

88

How NOT to Get Eaten

After reading the story, answer the questions.
Fill in the circle next to the correct answer.

1. What does a gliding frog do to escape from a predator?

   (a) It glides to another tree.

   (b) It wiggles its webbed feet.

   (c) It takes in water and swells up.

   (d) It sticks out its bright blue tongue.

2. This story is mainly about

   (a) how puffer fish can get big

   (b) how frogs glide with webbed feet

   (c) how some animals escape from predators

   (d) how a lizard wiggles its blue tongue

3. An animal that eats another animal

   (a) has spines

   (b) is a predator

   (c) likes surprises

   (d) is a bigger animal

4. Why do you think the lizard wiggles its tongue?

   (a) to make it swell up

   (b) to make it spread out

   (c) to make it bright blue

   (d) to make sure the predator sees it

5. Think about how the word **big** relates to **small**. Which words relate the same way?

big : small

   (a) dull : bright

   (b) webbed : feet

   (c) glide : wiggle

   (d) predator : escape

First in a Balloon

These are new words to practice.

Say each word 10 times.

✳ watch	✳ balloon
✳ crowd	✳ discovered
✳ rooster	✳ floated
✳ special	✳ straw

Choose one new word to write.

_____

- -

_____

First in a Balloon

The king of France had come. He had come to watch. Many people had come. They had all come to watch. There was a big crowd. They had all come to watch a sheep. They had all come to watch a rooster. They had all come to watch a duck. What was special about the sheep and the rooster? What was special about the duck? Why had a big crowd come to watch the animals?

The day was September 19th. The year was 1783. The animals were going to go up. They were going to go up in the air. They were going to ride in a hot-air balloon. They were going to be the first living things to ride in a hot-air balloon.

Joseph and Jacques Montgolfier made the balloon. Joseph and Jacques were brothers. They were from France. In 1782 they had discovered something. They had discovered that a large paper bag could rise in the air. The bag had to be filled with air. The air had to be heated. Hot air is lighter than cold air. Hot air rises. Our air is made of gases. Gases can change shape and size. When gases are heated, they spread out. The hot air spread out to fill the paper bag.

The brothers made bags out of cloth. The cloth was light. They filled the bags with heated air. The air was heated by burning straw and wool. They burned the straw and wool under the opening of the bag.

What did the sheep, rooster, and duck do? They went high into the air. They floated. They floated for eight minutes. They landed two miles (3.2 kilometers) away. Next, the brothers had people ride in their balloons. On November 21, 1783, the first men floated through the air in a balloon.

91

First in a Balloon

After reading the story, answer the questions.
Fill in the circle next to the correct answer.

1. This story is mainly about

   ⓐ a sheep

   ⓑ a big crowd

   ⓒ two brothers

   ⓓ hot air balloons

2. When did the two brothers discover something?

   ⓐ 1719

   ⓑ 1721

   ⓒ 1782

   ⓓ 1783

3. Why do you think the brothers sent up animals first?

   ⓐ The king liked animals.

   ⓑ They wanted to make sure it was safe.

   ⓒ The brothers wanted to go up in a bigger balloon.

   ⓓ The crowd wanted to watch a sheep, rooster, and duck.

4. Think about how the word **brother** relates to **boy**. Which words relate in the same way?

   | brother : boy |

   ⓐ sister : girl

   ⓑ people : crowd

   ⓒ rooster : animal

   ⓓ balloon : floats

5. When you discover something, you

   ⓐ float in the air

   ⓑ heat or burn something

   ⓒ fill a bag with heated air

   ⓓ find or learn something new

Why Pant?

These are new words to practice.

Say each word 10 times.

* pant

* exercise

* gasp

* muscles

* breathe

* energy

* oxygen

* glucose

Choose one new word to write.

_____

- -

_____

Why Pant?

Think about running. You can run fast. You can run fast when you play games. You can run fast in a race. What happens when you run fast? What happens when you play running games? What happens when you run a fast race? You begin to pant. You begin to gasp. You breathe with quick, deep breaths.

Why do you pant? Why do you gasp? Why do you breathe with quick, deep breaths? You pant when you need something. What do you need? You need oxygen. Oxygen is a gas. It is a gas in our air. We take in oxygen when we breathe.

We breathe faster when we pant. We take in more air with each breath, too. We take in more oxygen. We get more oxygen faster. We get the oxygen we need. When we get enough oxygen, we stop panting. We breathe slower. We do not gasp for air.

Why do we need more oxygen? Why do we need to pant so that we take in more air? Running is work. Running is a kind of exercise. Exercise is work. Our muscles work when we exercise. They work making our bones move. It takes energy to work. It takes energy to run. It takes energy to exercise. Our muscles need energy. How do they get it?

Our muscles get energy from sugar. The sugar is special. It is a special kind. It is called glucose. We get glucose from food. Our muscles need something to use glucose. They need oxygen. Glucose cannot be used for energy unless there is oxygen. Panting gets us more oxygen. Panting makes it so we can use more glucose. Panting makes it so we get more energy.

Why Pant?

**After reading the story, answer the questions.
Fill in the circle next to the correct answer.**

1. When you pant

   ⓐ you breathe slower and take in less air

   ⓑ you breathe faster and take in less air

   ⓒ you breathe slower and take in more air

   ⓓ you breathe faster and take in more air

2. Where do we get glucose?

   ⓐ from food

   ⓑ from oxygen

   ⓒ from energy

   ⓓ from exercise

3. This story is mainly about

   ⓐ why we pant

   ⓑ why we exercise

   ⓒ why oxygen is a gas

   ⓓ why glucose is special

4. What might take the most energy?

   ⓐ sitting

   ⓑ reading

   ⓒ jumping

   ⓓ sleeping

5. Think about how the word **slow** relates to **fast**. Which words relate in the same way?

slow : fast

   ⓐ pant : gasp

   ⓑ begin : stop

   ⓒ breathe : air

   ⓓ sugar : glucose

Maria's Comet

These are new words to practice.

Say each word 10 times.

* prize

* medal

* comet

* telescope

* travel

* steam

* vapor

* American

Choose one new word to write.

_____

- -

_____

Maria's Comet

The King of Denmark said, "I will give a prize." The prize was a gold medal. The prize was for the first person to see a new comet. The new comet could not be seen by the naked eye. It had to be seen by using a telescope.

A comet is a ball. It is a ball of ice and dust. Some comets are small. They are as small as a house. Some comets are big. They are miles (kilometers) across. Comets travel. They travel through space. Some comets orbit our sun. They go around our sun.

Some comets have tails. What are the tails? Where do they come from? The sun is hot. If a comet travels close to the sun, part of it melts. The sun's heat melts some ice. The ice turns into steam. It turns into water vapor. Ice is solid water. Steam or water vapor is a gas. It is water in the form of a gas.

The water vapor makes a glowing cloud. It makes a long, glowing tail. The tail is behind the comet. It points away from the sun. The tail follows the comet as it travels through space.

No American had won a gold medal. No woman had ever won a gold medal. Then, in 1847, Maria Mitchell became the first. She was the first American. She was the first woman. How did Maria know it was a comet? How did she know it was new? Maria worked hard. She studied the stars. She looked through a telescope for hours and hours. She knew the stars as well as she knew the streets around her home. When she saw the comet, she knew it had not been there before. It had to be new.

Maria's Comet

After reading the story, answer the questions.
Fill in the circle next to the correct answer.

1. This story is mainly about

   ⓐ Maria

   ⓑ comets

   ⓒ the King of Denmark

   ⓓ how to win a gold medal

2. Water vapor is a

   ⓐ gas

   ⓑ solid

   ⓒ comet

   ⓓ liquid

3. Think about how the word **ice** relates to **solid**. Which words relate in the same way?

ice : solid

   ⓐ comet : tail

   ⓑ prize : medal

   ⓒ telescope : look

   ⓓ water vapor : gas

4. What is true about a comet's tail?

   ⓐ It is new.

   ⓑ It follows the sun.

   ⓒ It points away from the sun.

   ⓓ It can only be seen using a telescope.

5. Why was Maria able to find the new comet?

   ⓐ She knew how to study for hours and hours.

   ⓑ She knew that some comets did not have tails.

   ⓒ She knew what the stars around her looked like.

   ⓓ She knew the King of Denmark was giving a prize.

The Largest Land Animal

These are new words to practice.

Say each word 10 times.

✳ animal	✳ trunk
✳ larger	✳ flexible
✳ brain	✳ tusks
✳ elephant	✳ blood

Choose one new word to write.

_____

- -

_____

The Largest Land Animal

One animal is very big. It lives on land. It is the largest land animal. It has a big head. Its head is larger than any other land animal's. Its brain is big. Its brain is larger than any other land animal's. It has a big nose. It is long. Its nose is longer than any other animal's. Can you name the animal?

It is the elephant. An elephant's nose is called a trunk. A trunk is very strong. It is so strong it can lift a big log. The trunk is very flexible. When something is flexible, it bends easily. It bends and does not break. The trunk is so flexible that an elephant can pick a flower.

Elephants can swim. They are good swimmers. Often, they swim underwater. They stick their trunks out as they swim. They breathe through their trunks. They can swim like this for a long time. They can swim far.

An elephant has two tusks. Tusks are teeth. The teeth are long. The teeth are large. An elephant uses its tusks to find food. It uses its tusks to find water, too. To find roots, an elephant digs in the ground. To find soft wood, an elephant opens tree trunks. To find water, an elephant digs in dry riverbeds. An elephant uses its tusks for all these things.

An elephant has two ears. The ears are big. Just one ear can weigh 110 pounds (50 kilograms)! Ears help an elephant stay cool. How do big ears help? Blood flows through the ears. When it is warm, the elephant flaps its ears. This cools the ears. This cools the blood flowing in the ears, too. The cooled blood flows back. It flows back to the rest of the elephant. It cools the elephant.

The Largest Land Animal

**After reading the story, answer the questions.
Fill in the circle next to the correct answer.**

1. When something is flexible,

   (a) it flows

   (b) it bends

   (a) it is long

   (b) it is strong

2. This story is mainly about

   (a) tusks

   (b) cooling blood

   (c) one land animal

   (d) an elephant's trunk

3. What is not true about elephants?

   (a) They are the best swimmers.

   (b) They are the largest land animals.

   (c) They have the longest nose of any animal.

   (d) They have the biggest brain of all the land animals.

4. Why does an elephant flap its ears?

   (a) to find water

   (b) to cool blood

   (c) to open tree trunks

   (d) to breathe underwater

5. Think about how the word **warm** relates to **cool**. Which words relate in the same way?

warm : cool

   (a) ear : flap

   (b) dig : tusk

   (c) nose : trunk

   (d) large : small

Raining Toads

These are new words to practice.

Say each word 10 times.

✳ funnel	✳ tornado
✳ clouds	✳ inland
✳ columns	✳ waterspout
✳ twist	✳ objects

Choose one new word to write.

_____

- -

_____

102

Raining Toads

One day it rained. It rained in France. It did not rain water. It rained toads! Toads fell from the sky. How could this be? How could toads fall from the sky? How could it rain toads in France?

Funnel clouds are columns of air. They are shaped like funnels. The air spins. The air spins fast. Funnel clouds twist down from thunderstorms. Sometimes they twist down to the ground. When a funnel cloud reaches the ground, it is called a tornado. Tornados are spinning winds.

Most tornados happen away from water. They happen inland. But some tornados happen over water. They form over rivers. They form over lakes. They form over oceans. Tornados that form over water are called waterspouts.

Tornados suck up warm air. Waterspouts suck up something else, too. They suck up water. They are columns of air and water. They spin fast. They can reach high into the sky. One waterspout was very big. It was over 1 mile (1.6 kilometers) high! Tornados pick up objects sometimes. The objects are picked up in the fast winds. Later, the objects are dropped.

Waterspouts pick up objects, too. Later, they are dropped. Fish have been picked up. Fish have been carried high in the air. They have been carried away from water. Then, they were dropped. When the fish were dropped, they fell from the sky. They landed on dry ground. They landed inland. Toads have been picked up, too. A lot of toads were picked up in France. They were carried high in the air. They were carried in the fast, spinning wind. Later, they were dropped. They fell from the sky. When they fell, it rained toads!

Raining Toads

After reading the story, answer the questions.
Fill in the circle next to the correct answer.

1. A funnel cloud becomes a tornado when it

   (a) sucks up warm air

   (b) happens over water

   (c) twists down to the ground

   (d) picks up objects and drops them

2. This story is mainly about

   (a) tornados in France

   (b) toads and waterspouts

   (c) the day it rained toads

   (d) objects in funnel clouds

3. Which statement is true?

   (a) All waterspouts are tornados.

   (b) All tornados are waterspouts.

   (c) All funnel clouds become tornados.

   (d) All toads are sucked up into waterspouts.

4. All waterspouts suck up

   (a) toads and water

   (b) objects and toads

   (c) warm air and water

   (d) warm air and objects

5. Think about how the word **carried** relates to **dropped**. Which words relate in the same way?

carried : dropped

   (a) up : down

   (b) rain : water

   (c) spin : twist

   (d) tornado : wind

Hot and Cold on Mercury

These are new words to practice.

Say each word 10 times.

✳ Earth	✳ temperature
✳ planet	✳ boiling
✳ Mercury	✳ craters
✳ daytime	✳ direct

Choose one new word to write.

_____

- -

_____

Hot and Cold on Mercury

We live on Earth. Earth is a planet. Our planet goes around the Sun. The Sun warms the Earth. It warms our land. It warms our air. It warms our water. Other planets go around the Sun. The Sun warms these planets, too.

Mercury is a planet. It is the closest planet to our Sun. It is closer to the Sun than Earth. Mercury is so near the Sun that it gets very hot. Daytime temperatures are very hot. In the daytime, it is hotter than boiling water! In fact, it can be four times hotter than boiling water!

What happens to the temperature at night? At night, Mercury gets very cold. It is far, far below freezing. Mercury has lots of craters. A crater is a hole. It is shaped like a bowl. Some craters are deep. They are so deep that sunlight cannot reach the bottom. Sunlight cannot warm the bottom of the craters. It is very cold. The temperature day and night is far, far below freezing in the craters.

Think about our days. Do you think our days are long? A day is the time it takes Earth to spin around once. Our days are 24 hours long. A day on Mercury is long. It is 59 Earth days long! Why are the days long? Mercury spins slowly. It spins slower than Earth. It takes 59 Earth days for Mercury to spin around once!

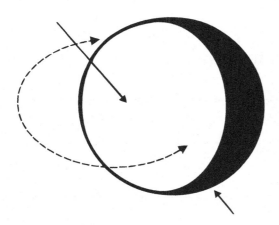

At night, we do not face the sun. The Earth has turned. It has spun around. We do not feel direct sunlight. We do not feel as much warmth. Think about Mercury. It spins slowly. Its nights are very long. It does not feel direct sunlight for a long time. This is why it gets so cold at night.

Hot and Cold on Mercury

After reading the story, answer the questions.
Fill in the circle next to the correct answer.

1. How many days are there on Earth for one day on Mercury?

    (a) 24
    (b) 29
    (c) 54
    (d) 59

2. From the story, you can tell that

    (a) direct sunlight is cold
    (b) Earth is hotter than Mercury
    (c) it gets very hot close to the sun
    (d) night and day temperatures are the same

3. This story is mainly about

    (a) planets
    (b) day and night
    (c) sunlight and craters
    (d) temperature on Mercury

4. A crater is a

    (a) hole shaped like a bowl
    (b) planet that spins very slowly
    (c) hole where sunlight cannot reach
    (d) planet that goes around the Earth

5. Think about how the word **boiling** relates to **freezing**. Which words relate in the same way?

    boiling : freezing

    (a) hot : cold
    (b) spin : spun
    (c) night : crater
    (d) Earth : planet

What Do You Need?

These are new words to practice.

Say each word 10 times.

✳ water	✳ equal
✳ vegetables	✳ two-thirds
✳ divide	✳ body
✳ break	✳ replace

Choose one new word to write.

_____

- -

_____

What Do You Need?

You need it. Animals need it. Plants need it. You need it to live. What is it? It is water. All plants and animals need water to live. How do plants get water? They use their roots. How do animals get water? The same way you do. Animals drink water. They get water from food.

We eat plants. Plants are mostly water. We eat vegetables. Vegetables are mostly water. Think of a vegetable. Now divide it. When you divide something, you break it into parts. Divide the vegetable into 10 parts. The parts should be equal. They should be the same. How many parts will be water? Nine parts will be water! Only one part will not be water. Most vegetables are about nine-tenths water!

Think of rice. Now divide the rice. Break it into three parts. The parts should be equal. They should be the same. Two of the parts will be water! Rice is two-thirds water. Think of chicken. Now divide it into three equal parts. Two parts will be water! Chicken is two-thirds water.

How about you? Are you mostly water? Yes, you are! Divide your body into three equal parts. Two of the parts will be water! Your body weight is about two-thirds water! Your blood has water. Your tears have water. Your bones have water. Your skin has water. All your body parts have water.

You lose water every day. How do you lose water? You lose it when you go to the bathroom. You lose it when you sweat. You lose it when you breathe out. You can lose up to six pints (3 liters) of water a day. You need to replace it. You can replace it by drinking. You can replace it by eating foods with water.

What Do You Need?

**After reading the story, answer the questions.
Fill in the circle next to the correct answer.**

1. Your body weight is about how much water?

   (a) one-third

   (b) one-tenth

   (c) two-thirds

   (d) nine-tenths

2. This story is mainly about

   (a) how you lose water

   (b) how you need and get water

   (c) what body parts have water

   (d) how much water is in vegetables

3. Which statement is true?

   (a) Vegetables are mostly water.

   (b) Your bones do not have water.

   (c) We cannot lose water at night.

   (d) Plants get water by eating food.

4. When you replace something, you

   (a) lose it

   (b) put it back

   (c) breathe it out

   (d) divide it into equal parts

5. Think about how the word **drink** relates to **water**. Which words relate the same way?

   | **drink : water** |

   (a) eat : food

   (b) lose : need

   (c) equal : same

   (d) plant : root

All About Hurricanes

These are new words to practice.

Say each word 10 times.

* hurricanes   * oceans

* storms   * cyclone

* powerful   * typhoon

* tropical   * warn

Choose one new word to write.

_____

- -

_____

All About Hurricanes

Hurricanes are storms. They are big. They are powerful. They are strong. They are the biggest most powerful storms on Earth. They start over water. The water must be warm. It cannot be cold. Hurricanes start over tropical oceans. Tropical oceans lie close to the equator. Close to the equator, the water is warm. It is not cold.

Warm water heats up air. It heats up air just above it. When air heats up, it becomes lighter. It rises. Cool air moves in. Cool air fills in where the warm air was. All this movement causes winds. Sometimes the air rises very fast. Fast winds start. The fast winds start to spin. A spinning storm starts. When is the storm a hurricane? It is a hurricane when the winds go very fast. They must go about 74 miles (120 kilometers) per hour.

Hurricanes have many names. In some places they are called cyclones. In some places they are called typhoons. Hurricanes are storms. Cyclones are storms. Typhoons are storms. They are all the same kind of storm.

A hurricane does not stay in one place. It moves. It can move miles over the ocean. It moves like a spinning top. When does it stop? It stops when it moves to a new place. The place has cooler water. Or, it has cooler land. Without warm water, a hurricane will die.

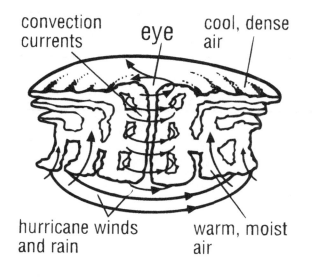

convection currents   eye   cool, dense air

hurricane winds and rain   warm, moist air

Scientists study storms. They study when storms happen. They study where. Scientists now know hurricanes happen every year. Scientists see where storms start at sea. They follow the storms. They track them. They see where the storms go. They see when the storms turn into hurricanes. They warn people. They warn people at sea. They warn people on land. They help people be safe.

All About Hurricanes

After reading the story, answer the questions.
Fill in the circle next to the correct answer.

1. Why do hurricanes start over tropical oceans?

   (a) Tropical oceans lie close to land.

   (b) Tropical oceans lie close to typhoons.

   (c) Tropical oceans lie close to cold water.

   (d) Tropical oceans lie close to the equator.

2. What is not true about hurricanes?

   (a) They stay in one place.

   (b) They start over warm water.

   (c) They move like a spinning top.

   (d) They are the same kind of storm as typhoons.

3. This story is mainly about

   (a) storms

   (b) fast winds

   (c) hurricanes

   (d) scientists

4. Why do hurricanes die?

   (a) They move away from land.

   (b) They move away from cold water.

   (c) They move away from fast winds.

   (d) They move away from warm water.

5. Think about how the word **warm** relates to **cool**. Which words relate in the same way?

warm : cool

   (a) warn : tell

   (b) stay : move

   (c) spin : rise

   (d) cyclone : typhoon

Into a Crocodile's Mouth

These are new words to practice.
Say each word 10 times.

* crocodile   * attach

* bird   * gums

* afraid   * enemies

* leeches   * keen

Choose one new word to write.

_____

- -

_____

Into a Crocodile's Mouth

The Nile crocodile is big. It lives in Africa. It has big teeth. It is strong. The crocodile can move fast. It is a good, fast swimmer. It eats fish. It eats animals. It eats with its big, strong teeth.

One bird is not afraid of the crocodile. The bird is not afraid of the crocodile's big, strong teeth. Fish are afraid. Animals are afraid. People are afraid, too. Why isn't the bird afraid?

The Nile crocodile lives in water. The water is warm. The water is muddy. Leeches live in the water. Leeches are small. They look like worms. They get in the crocodile's mouth. They attach themselves to the crocodile's gums. They stick to the gums. Then, they suck the crocodile's blood. The crocodile cannot get rid of the leeches. The leeches are stuck on. They are attached.

The crocodile opens its mouth. It opens it wide. It shows its teeth. It shows its gums. It shows its tongue. The bird goes up to the crocodile. It hops into its mouth! The bird picks at the leeches. It eats the leeches. It eats other pests, too. The bird cleans the crocodile's teeth. It cleans its gums. It cleans its tongue. The crocodile gets clean. The bird gets food.

The bird is safe with the crocodile. It is safe from its enemies. The bird's enemies are afraid to come near. They are afraid of the crocodile. The bird helps the crocodile stay safe, too. The bird has keen eyes. When something has keen eyes, it can see well. With its keen eyes, the bird can spot danger. It can see people coming. The bird calls out. The calls warn the crocodile. The crocodile can swim away. It can dive to safety.

Into a Crocodile's Mouth

After reading the story, answer the questions.
Fill in the circle next to the correct answer.

1. This story is mainly about

   ⓐ crocodiles

   ⓑ a cleaning bird

   ⓒ how two animals get along

   ⓓ how birds keep crocodiles safe

2. Where do some leeches attach themselves?

   ⓐ to blood

   ⓑ to warm, muddy water

   ⓒ to a crocodile's gums

   ⓓ to a crocodile's teeth

3. Think about how the word in relates to out. Which words relate in the same way?

in : out

   ⓐ hop : jump

   ⓑ big : small

   ⓒ swim : dive

   ⓓ teeth : clean

4. If you have keen hearing, you

   ⓐ can't see

   ⓑ can't hear

   ⓒ can see well

   ⓓ can hear well

5. Why is the bird safe with the crocodile?

   ⓐ The bird can hop into the crocodile's mouth.

   ⓑ The bird's enemies are afraid of the crocodile.

   ⓒ The leeches will only attach themselves to a crocodile.

   ⓓ The crocodile will warn the bird when its enemies are near.

The Snowflake Man

These are new words to practice.

Say each word 10 times.

* camera   * branches

* pictures   * shadows

* snowflakes   * lens

* microscope   * grasshoppers

Choose one new word to write.

_____

- -

_____

The Snowflake Man

Bentley wanted a camera. The camera was big. It cost a lot. It cost as much as ten cows. Bentley's parents did not have a lot of money. Still, they gave it to him. Bentley was seventeen-years-old. Why did he want the camera that cost so much?

Bentley was born in 1865. He was born on a farm. The farm was in Vermont. It is cold in Vermont. It snows a lot. It snows about 120 inches (3 meters) a year. Bentley liked snow. He liked it a lot. He wanted to take pictures. He wanted to take pictures of snowflakes.

The camera had a microscope. A microscope is used to look at tiny things. It makes things look bigger. The microscope could make things look 3,600 times bigger! Bentley knew that no two snowflakes are alike. He knew that snowflakes have six branches. The six branches are all alike. Bentley wanted other people to know this, too. How could he show them? He could show them pictures.

At first, the pictures did not come out. They were like shadows. Bentley did not give up. He got cold. Still, he worked. It took Bentley two years to find a way. He had to use a small lens. A lens lets in light. Bentley had to leave the lens open. Sometimes he left the lens open for a minute-and-a -half. At last, Bentley's pictures did not look like shadows. The pictures were put in a book.

Bentley took other pictures. He took pictures of grasshoppers. Dew was on the grasshoppers. Why did the grasshoppers stay still? They were tied! They were tied to a branch! Bentley tied them at night. In the morning, he took their picture. Then, he would let them go.

The Snowflake Man

After reading the story, answer the questions.
Fill in the circle next to the correct answer.

1. This story is mainly about

   (a) grasshoppers

   (b) snow in Vermont

   (c) a man who took pictures

   (d) a camera with a microscope

2. How many branches does a snowflake have?

   (a) two

   (b) six

   (c) seventeen

   (d) 3,600

3. Think about how the word **tiny** relates to **big**. Which words relate in the same way?

tiny : big

   (a) lens : open

   (b) snow : cold

   (c) stay : tied

   (d) first : last

4. What does a lens do?

   (a) It lets in light.

   (b) It makes a shadow.

   (c) It takes a picture.

   (d) It makes things look bigger.

5. What made Bentley's camera cost a lot?

   (a) It was big.

   (b) It took pictures.

   (c) It had a microscope in it.

   (d) It cost as much as ten cows.

Snow on the Equator

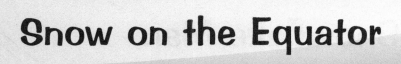

These are new words to practice.

Say each word 10 times.

* Kenya   * globe

* equator   * mountains

* imaginary   * oxygen

* divide   * tanks

Choose one new word to write.

_____

- -

_____

Snow on the Equator

Kenya is a country. It is in Africa. The equator runs through Kenya. The equator is a line. It is imaginary. It is not a real line. We use the imaginary line. We use it to divide the globe. The equator is in the middle. It divides the globe into two parts.

It is hot on the equator. It is hot in Kenya. It is hot in Kenya, but there is snow. Snow is cold. How can there be cold snow in hot Kenya? How can there be snow near the equator? Snow in Kenya is high up. It is only on the top of high mountains. It is on top of Mt. Kenya. Mt. Kenya is high. It is the highest mountain in Kenya. Why doesn't the snow melt? Why doesn't snow melt on the top of high mountains?

Air is all around us. Our air is made of different gases. Our air gets thinner the higher you go. The air is very thin at the top of high mountains. Thin air gets very cold. It gets very cold at night. It gets so cold that snow does not melt.

Mt. Everest is a mountain. It is high. It is the highest mountain in the world. The air is very thin at the top of Mt. Everest. It is so thin that a helicopter cannot take flight. Climbers bring oxygen. The oxygen is in tanks. Climbers breathe oxygen from the tanks.

What is a snow line? A snow line is a place. It is the place where a mountain begins to be covered in snow. Plants cannot grow above the snow line. It is too cold. Plants need water. Plants cannot take in snow and ice. Plants cannot take in frozen water.

Snow on the Equator

After reading the story, answer the questions.
Fill in the circle next to the correct answer.

1. This story is mainly about
   - (a) air around us
   - (b) a country in Africa
   - (c) snow on high mountains
   - (d) plants near the snow line

2. Snow doesn't melt on the top of Mt. Kenya because
   - (a) the air is thin
   - (b) there are no plants
   - (c) it is on the equator
   - (d) it is the highest mountain

3. Think about how the word **hot** relates to **cold**. Which words relate in the same way?

hot : cold

   - (a) equator : line
   - (b) Kenya : Africa
   - (c) imaginary : real
   - (d) mountain : snow line

4. From the story you can tell that snow and ice are
   - (a) frozen water
   - (b) good for plants
   - (c) not near the equator
   - (d) made of different gases

5. What is not true above the snow line?
   - (a) The air is thin.
   - (b) Plants can grow.
   - (c) It is cold at night.
   - (d) Snow covers the mountain.

Flowers on the Move

These are new words to practice.

Say each word 10 times.

* young * follow

* sunflower * cultivate

* sunlight * Europe

* energy * brought

Choose one new word to write.

_____

- -

_____

Flowers on the Move

The sun rises. It is morning. Young sunflower plants do something in the morning. They turn. They bend. They turn and bend to the east. Why do the young plants turn to the east?

Sunflower plants are big. They grow very tall. Some plants grow 20 feet (6 meters) tall! Plants need food. Big, tall plants need lots of food. Plants make their food. Plants need sunlight to make food. They use the energy in sunlight. They turn the energy into food. Big, tall plants need lots of sunlight. They need lots of sunlight to make lots of food.

Young sunflower plants need lots of energy. They need lots of sunlight. The plants turn to the sun. In the morning, they turn to the sun so they can get more sunlight. The plants follow the sun. All day, the sun moves across the sky. It moves from east to west. All day, young sunflowers follow the sun. They bend from east to west. All day, they turn to get more sun.

Long ago, sunflowers were only in North America. They were wild. Over 4,000 years ago, people started to cultivate them. When you cultivate a plant, you help it to grow. You take care of it. People used the plant. They ate its seeds. They made oil. They made paint. They made medicine.

Travelers came to North America. They came from Europe. They saw the sunflowers. They wanted to grow them, too. They brought them back to Europe. They brought them back in the 1500s. In the 1700s, sunflower plants were brought to Russia. Lots of sunflowers are cultivated in Russia today. They are used for food. They are used to make oil. Long ago, sunflowers moved around the world. Today, young plants still move. They turn east to west!

Flowers on the Move

After reading the story, answer the questions.
Fill in the circle next to the correct answer.

1. This story is mainly about

   ⓐ sunflowers

   ⓑ plants that move

   ⓒ cultivated flowers

   ⓓ how plants make food

2. Why do young sunflower plants turn east to west?

   ⓐ They are cultivated.

   ⓑ They are used to make food and oil.

   ⓒ They need to get as much sunlight as they can.

   ⓓ They need more energy if they turn east to west.

3. Which answer is in the correct order of where sunflowers grew first?

   ⓐ North America, Europe, Russia

   ⓑ Europe, North America, Russia

   ⓒ North America, Russia, Europe

   ⓓ Russia, Europe, North America

4. Think about how the word **young** relates to **old**. Which words relate in the same way?

young : old

   ⓐ follow : sun

   ⓑ travel : move

   ⓒ planted : grow

   ⓓ cultivated : wild

5. How long ago did people start to cultivate sunflowers?

   ⓐ in the 1500s

   ⓑ in the 1700s

   ⓒ over 1,500 years ago

   ⓓ over 4,000 years ago

Penguins

These are new words to practice.

Say each word 10 times.

* penguins	* blubber
* freezing	* tightly
* warm-blooded	* packed
* layers	* escape

Choose one new word to write.

_____

- -

_____

126

Penguins

Penguins live in cold places. How do penguins stay warm in cold places? How do penguins keep from freezing? Penguins are warm-blooded. When something is warm-blooded, it makes heat inside its body. It does not need the sun to warm it.

Penguins have several layers. The layers keep heat in. First, a penguin has a layer of blubber. Blubber is a thick layer of fat. Blubber helps to keep the heat in. The next layer is skin. Skin helps keep heat in, too. A penguin's feathers make up the last layer. The feathers are tightly packed. The penguins use the feathers to make another layer. They use the feathers to trap a layer of air. The layer of air is between the skin and the feathers.

Sometimes, penguins need to cool down! They get too hot with all their layers. They need to cool down when the weather warms up. Penguins use their feathers to cool down. Think of a door. Close a door tight. No air can get in. No heat can escape. Open a door. Air can go out. Heat can escape. Penguin feathers are like a door.

Remember that penguin feathers are tightly packed. When the feathers are held tight against a penguin's body, they are like a closed door. No heat can escape. When the feathers are fluffed, they are like an open door. Heat can escape. A penguin can cool down.

Some penguins do not make nests. The penguins keep their eggs safe by carrying them! They carry them on their feet. They carry the baby penguins on their feet, too! How do the penguins keep their eggs and babies warm? They can cover them. They can cover them with a flap of skin. The flap of skin keeps the eggs and babies from freezing.

Penguins

After reading the story, answer the questions.
Fill in the circle next to the correct answer.

1. This story is mainly about
   - (a) layers
   - (b) feathers
   - (c) penguins
   - (d) staying warm

2. What do penguins that do not make nests use to keep their eggs and babies warm?
   - (a) skin
   - (b) layers
   - (c) blubber
   - (d) feathers

3. What order could a penguin's layers go in?
   - (a) skin, blubber, air, feathers
   - (b) blubber, skin, air, feathers
   - (c) blubber, skin, feathers, air
   - (d) air, blubber, skin, feathers

4. Think about how the word **freezing** relates to **cold**. Which words relate in the same way?

   | **freezing: cold** |

   - (a) warming : heat
   - (b) carrying : eggs
   - (c) covering : skin
   - (d) opening : escape

5. Tightly packed feathers
   - (a) are fluffed
   - (b) let heat escape
   - (c) are like an open door
   - (d) do not let heat escape

Mud from the Sky

These are new words to practice.

Say each word 10 times.

* radio   * ashes

* volcano   * clouds

* erupted   * settle

* island   * scientists

Choose one new word to write.

_____

- - - - - - - - - - - - - - - - - -

_____

Mud from the Sky

Tess turned the radio on. She wanted to listen. She wanted to listen to the news. Tess heard, "Mud is falling from the sky." Tess knew rain fell from the sky. She knew snow fell from the sky. She knew hail fell from the sky. She did not know mud fell from the sky. Could mud really fall from the sky? Could the news on the radio really be true?

The news was true. Mud really was falling from the sky. The year was 1991. A volcano erupted. When something erupts, it breaks out. The erupting volcano was on an island. The island was in the Philippines. When the volcano erupted, dust and ashes blew into the air. The dust and ashes made clouds. The clouds were big. The clouds were black. The clouds blocked out the sun.

Dust and ashes began to settle. When something settles, it comes to rest. The dust and ashes settled on cars. It settled on trees. It settled on streets. It settled on houses. It settled on everything.

Before all the dust and ashes had settled, it began to rain. The rain made the dust and ashes in the air wet. The dust and ashes turned to mud. The news on the radio was true. Mud was falling from the sky.

Scientists study volcanoes. When a volcano erupts, scientists look at the dust and ashes. They study the clouds. They see how long the dust stays in the air. They see how far the wind blows it. The dust goes high into the air. It stays high in the air for a long time. The wind blows it far. Scientists have found dust from some volcanoes half way around the world!

Mud from the Sky

**After reading the story, answer the questions.
Fill in the circle next to the correct answer.**

1. What made mud fall from the sky?

   (a) wind blowing clouds of dust and ashes

   (b) dust and ashes settling on everything

   (c) dust and ashes erupting from a volcano

   (d) rain mixed with dust and ashes in the air

2. If you settle on an island,

   (a) you block out the sun.

   (b) you stay high in the air.

   (c) you break out from the island.

   (d) you rest or live on an island.

3. This story is mainly about

   (a) erupting volcanoes

   (b) what scientists study

   (c) mud falling from the sky

   (d) an island in the Philippines

4. What year did the volcano erupt?

   (a) 1991

   (b) 1993

   (c) 1995

   (d) 1997

5. Think about how the word **read** relates to **book**. Which words relate in the same way?

read : book

   (a) dust : ashes

   (b) listen : radio

   (c) clouds : volcano

   (d) scientists : study

The Biggest Rain Forest

These are new words to practice.

Say each word 10 times.

* forest

* tropical

* roof

* canopy

* branches

* Amazon

* toucan

* beaks

Choose one new word to write.

The Biggest Rain Forest

A forest is made of a lot of trees. The trees grow close to each other. One type of a forest is a tropical rain forest. It is wet all year round. It is warm. The tops of the trees grow close together. They form a roof over the forest floor.

The roof is called a canopy. A canopy is a layer of treetops. A canopy can be 20 feet (6 meters) thick. Lots of animals live in the canopy. Lots of plants live in the canopy, too. Lots of animals and plants never touch the ground. They spend their whole lives in the canopy.

Some plants are air plants. They grow on tree branches. The roots of air plants do not grow in the ground. The roots hang in the air. How do air plants get water? They get water from the air. How do air plants get food? They get food from leaves and molds. The leaves and molds are on the tree branches.

The biggest tropical rain forest is in South America. It is called the Amazon rain forest. The Amazon River runs through it. The river is big. Only one river is longer. Only the Nile is longer. The Nile River is not in South America. It is in Egypt. The Nile is longer, but the Amazon has more water. It has two-thirds of all the fresh water in the world!

Toucans are birds. They live in the Amazon rain forest. They have big beaks. Some toucans have beaks that are a third of the length of their body! The beaks are light. They are strong. They are bright, too. They are brightly colored. Toucans use their beaks to pick fruit. They even use their beaks to toss fruit to each other!

The Biggest Rain Forest

**After reading the story, answer the questions.
Fill in the circle next to the correct answer.**

1. This story is mainly about

    ⓐ forests

    ⓑ toucans

    ⓒ air plants

    ⓓ rain forests

2. The roof of the rain forest is called the

    ⓐ Amazon

    ⓑ canopy

    ⓒ tropical

    ⓓ tree branch

3. How do air plants get water?

    ⓐ from the air

    ⓑ from the ground

    ⓒ from their roots

    ⓓ from tree branches

4. Think about how the word **plant** relates to **garden**. Which words relate in the same way?

    | **plant : garden** |

    ⓐ bird : beak

    ⓑ river : long

    ⓒ tree : forest

    ⓓ branch : tree

5. What is not true about the Amazon River?

    ⓐ It is in South America.

    ⓑ It is the longest in the world.

    ⓒ It runs through the Amazon rain forest.

    ⓓ It has two-thirds of all the fresh water in the world.

A Lucky Accident

These are new words to practice.
Say each word 10 times.

* eraser   * elastic

* bottom   * stretched

* tennis   * accident

* rubber   * sulfur

Choose one new word to write.

_____

- -

_____

A Lucky Accident

Think of a tire. Think of a ball. Think of an eraser. Think of the bottom of a tennis shoe. Think of all these things. Now, can you think of what these things have in common? What makes the tire and the ball alike? What makes the eraser and the bottom of a tennis shoe alike? The tire and the ball are made of rubber. An eraser and the bottom of a tennis shoe are made out of rubber, too.

Rubber is springy. It is elastic. When something is elastic, it can be stretched. After it is stretched, it is able to spring back into shape. We can get rubber from plants. Long ago, people used rubber from plants. They used it to make raincoats!

Today we can make rubber. We make rubber by mixing things together. We use rubber we make and rubber from plants for many things. We use rubber for many things because of an accident. The accident was lucky.

Rubber used to melt. It would melt in the hot sun. Rubber used to crack. It would crack in the cold. A man wanted to make rubber better. The man's name was Charles Goodyear. Charles wanted to make rubber more elastic. He wanted to make it stronger. He mixed things into the rubber. He mixed ink. He mixed soup. He mixed oil. He mixed cheese. Nothing worked. The rubber still melted. It still cracked.

One day Charles dropped some rubber. It was an accident. He dropped it into a pot. The pot was on the stove. The pot had sulfur in it. The heat and the sulfur did something to the rubber. Heat and sulfur changed the rubber. It made it more elastic. It made it stronger. It stopped it from melting. It stopped it from cracking.

A Lucky Accident

**After reading the story, answer the questions.
Fill in the circle next to the correct answer.**

1. This story is mainly about

   (a) rubber

   (b) accidents

   (c) Charles Goodyear

   (d) tires, balls, erasers, and the bottom of shoes

2. What does heat and sulfur do to rubber?

   (a) It makes it melt.

   (b) It makes it crack.

   (c) It makes it into oil.

   (d) It makes it stronger.

3. Think about how the word **hot** relates to **cold**. Which words relate in the same way?

   | hot : cold |

   (a) mix : add

   (b) top : bottom

   (c) strong : rubber

   (d) accident : lucky

4. When something is elastic, it

   (a) can be mixed

   (b) can be heated

   (c) can be stretched

   (d) can be made into a raincoat

5. From the story, you can tell that

   (a) We use rubber for many things.

   (b) Charles had lots of accidents.

   (c) We use rubber from plants for tires.

   (d) Charles knew to heat rubber and mix it with sulfur.

The Largest Hopper

These are new words to practice.

Say each word 10 times.

✳ kangaroos	✳ pouch
✳ mammals	✳ joey
✳ young	✳ Australia
✳ marsupials	✳ survive

Choose one new word to write.

_____

- - - - - - - - - - - - - - - - - -

_____

The Largest Hopper

Some animals hop. They jump. Can you think of some hopping animals?
Grasshoppers hop. Rabbits hop. You can hop, too! What is the largest hopper? What is the largest hopping animal? It is not a grasshopper. It is not a rabbit. It is not you. It is a kangaroo.

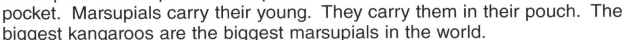

Kangaroos are mammals. Mammals have hair. Mammals feed their young milk. They are warm-blooded. Kangaroos are a special type of mammal. They are marsupials. Marsupials have a pouch. The pouch is like a pocket. Marsupials carry their young. They carry them in their pouch. The biggest kangaroos are the biggest marsupials in the world.

Baby kangaroos are called joeys. They are small. How small? They can be as small as a bumblebee! Joeys start out less than 1 inch (2.5 centimeters) long. As soon as the joey is born, it starts climbing. It climbs up to its mother's pouch. Its eyes are closed. It cannot hear. It has no fur. Its mother does not help.

How does a joey find its way? How does it climb? It finds its way by its sense of smell. The joey has claws. The claws are sharp. The sharp claws are on its front paws. The joey holds on to its mother's fur. It uses its sharp claws to hold on. The joey stays inside the pouch for six months. It drinks milk. It grows big. When it comes out, its eyes are open. It can hear. It has fur. It is ready to hop!

Kangaroos live in Australia. It is hot in Australia. Sometimes there is not much water. What do the kangaroos do? How do they survive? They survive by eating plants. They get water from plants. Sometimes they dig holes. Water comes up in the holes. Some kangaroos can go weeks without drinking water.

The Largest Hopper

After reading the story, answer the questions.
Fill in the circle next to the correct answer.

1. This story is mainly about
   - (a) hopping
   - (b) kangaroos
   - (c) Australia
   - (d) marsupials

2. When a joey is born,
   - (a) it can see
   - (b) it has fur
   - (c) it can hear
   - (d) it can climb

3. What statement is true?
   - (a) All mammals are marsupials.
   - (b) All marsupials are mammals.
   - (c) All mammals are hopping animals.
   - (d) All marsupials are hopping animals.

4. Think about how the word **kangaroo** relates to **joey**. Which words relate in the same way?

   | **kangaroo: joey** |

   - (a) dog : puppy
   - (b) kitten : cat
   - (c) baby : young
   - (d) water : drink

5. If you can survive,
   - (a) you can live
   - (b) you can dig holes
   - (c) you can eat plants
   - (d) you can drink water

Answer Sheet

Student Name: _____

Title of Reading Passage: _____

1. (a)   (b)   (c)   (d)
2. (a)   (b)   (c)   (d)
3. (a)   (b)   (c)   (d)
4. (a)   (b)   (c)   (d)
5. (a)   (b)   (c)   (d)

Student Name: _____

Title of Reading Passage: _____

1. (a)   (b)   (c)   (d)
2. (a)   (b)   (c)   (d)
3. (a)   (b)   (c)   (d)
4. (a)   (b)   (c)   (d)
5. (a)   (b)   (c)   (d)

Bibliography

Baker, Beth. *Sylvia Earle: Guardian of the Sea*. Lerner Publications Company, 2001.

Biel, Timothy Levi. *Zoobooks: Spiders*. Wildlife Education, Ltd., 1992.

Brust, Beth Wagner. *Zoobooks: Kangaroos*. Wildlife Education, Ltd., 1990.

Christian, Spencer, and Felix, Antonia. *Can It Really Rain Frogs?: the World's Strangest Weather Events*. John Wiley & Sons, Inc., 1997.

Fischer-Nagel, Heiderose and Andreas. *The Housefly*. Carolrhoda Books, Inc., 1990.

Foster, Ruth. *Take Five Minutes: Fascinating Facts About Geography*. Teacher Created Materials, Inc., 2003.

——. *Take Five Minutes: Fascinating Facts and Stories for Reading and Critical Thinking*. Teacher Created Materials, Inc., 2001.

Gallant, Roy A. *Glaciers*. Franklin Watts, Grolier Publishing, 1999.

Ganeri, Anita. *Explore the World of Exotic Rainforests*. Western Publishing Company, Inc., 1992.

Gormley, Beatrice. *Maria Mitchell: The Soul of an Astronomer*. William B. Eerdmans Publishing Company, 1995.

Hawkes, Nigel. *Mysteries of the Universe*. Copper Beech Books, The Millbrook Press, 2000.

Hipp, Andrew. *Sunflowers Inside and Out*. The Rosen Publishing Group, Inc., 2004.

Hirschmann, Kris. *The Octopus*. KidHaven Press, 2003.

Jenkins, Steve. *What Do You Do When Something Wants to Eat You?* Houghton Mifflin Company, 1997.

Johnson, Neil. *Fire & Silk: Flying in a Hot Air Balloon*. Little, Brown, and Company, 1991.

Mack, Lorrie. *Weather*. DK Publishing, Inc., 2004.

Martin, Jacqueline Briggs. *Snowflake Bentley*. Houghton Mifflin Company, 1998.

Miles, Lisa, and Smith, Alistair. *The Usborne Complete Book of Astronomy & Space*. Scholastic, Inc., 1998.

"Montgolfier, Joseph-Michel and Jacques-Etienne," *The New Encyclopedia Britannica Micropaedia, volume 8*, page 290. Encyclopedia Britannica, Inc., 1990.

Penny, Malcolm. *How Plants Grow*. Benchmark Books, Marshall Cavendish, 1997.

Pohl, Kathleen. *Sunflowers*. Raintree Publishers, 1987.

Royston, Angela. *Why Do Bruises Change Color? And Other Questions About Blood*. Heinemann Library, Reed Educational and Professional Publishing, 2003.

——. *Why Do I Sneeze? And Other Questions About Breathing*. Heinemann Library, Reed Educational and Professional Publishing, 2003.

Bibliography *(cont.)*

——. *Why Do I Vomit? And Other Questions About Digestion*. Heinemann Library, Reed Educational and Professional Publishing, 2003.

Silverstein, Alvin and Virginia, and Nunn, Laura Silverstein. *Symbiosis*. Twenty-First Century Books, 1998.

Spilsbury, Louise and Richard. *Howling Hurricanes*. Heinemann Library, Reed Elsevier, Inc., 2004.

——. *Terrifying Tornadoes.* Heinemann Library, Reed Elsevier, Inc., 2004.

Steele, Philip. *Deserts*. Carolrhoda Books, Inc., 1996.

Stewart, Melissa. *Life Without Light: A Journey to Earth's Dark Ecosystems.* Franklin Watts, Grolier Publishing, 1999.

Thompson, Brenda, and Giesen, Rosemary. *The Story of Steel*. Lerner Publications Company, 1977.

Tomecek, Stephen M. *Inventions that Changed the World*. Scholastic, Inc., 2003.

Weber, Belinda. *Animal Disguises.* Kingfisher, Houghton Mifflin Company, 2004.

Wexo, John Bonnett. *Zoobooks: Elephants.* Wildlife Education, Ltd., 1986.

——. *Zoobooks: Penguins.* Wildlife Education, Ltd., 1988.

——. *Zoobooks: Sharks.* Wildlife Education, Ltd., 1988.

Answer Key

Page 11—Sharks
1.D 2.C 3.B 4.C 5.A

Page 14—Something Fast
1.B 2.D 3.C 4.D 5.C

Page 17—The First Step on the Moon
1.c 2.c 3.d 4.a 5.b

Page 20—Eating Without Teeth
1.d 2.a 3.c 4.b 5.d

Page 23—All About Wind
1.c 2.a 3.c 4.a 5.d

Page 26—Seeds with Wings and Other Things
1.c 2.d 3.b 4.d 5.b

Page 29—Steel
1.c 2.b 3.a 4.b 5.d

Page 32—Animals Tricks
1.c 2.a 3.d 4.b 5.c

Page 35—Out of Air
1.d 2.a 3.a 4.b 5.c

Page 38—The Month of June—Summer or Winter?
1.c 2.b 3.b 4.d 5.d

Page 41—Leaf Detective
1.c 2.a 3.d 4.d 5.a

Page 44—Spiders
1.d 2.c 3.d 4.a 5.b

Page 47—Harder Than Bone
1.b 2.c 3.b 4.a 5.a

Page 50—Glacier: Ice on the Move
1.d 2.c 3.a 4.d 5.c

Page 53—Paper
1.b 2.b 3.c 4.d 5.a

Page 56—Creature in the Dark
1.a 2.b 3.c 4.a 5.c

Page 59—The Way the Wind Blows
1.a 2.d 3.a 4.d 5.b

Page 62—Tools in the Wild
1.b 2.c 3.b 4.d 5.d

Page 65—Dry Deserts
1.a 2.c 3.b 4.b 5.d

Page 68—Light and Dark
1.c 2.b 3.c 4.b 5.d

Page 71—Shoots Up, Roots Down
1.b 2.c 3.c 4.d 5.d

Page 74—Why Bruises Change Color
1.b 2.c 3.d 4.d 5.a

Page 77—An Old Story Made New
1.c 2.b 3.b 4.c 5.d

Page 80—Something Wrong
1.d 2.b 3.d 4.c 5.c

Page 83—How Men Were Saved
1.d 2.b 3.c 4.c 5.b

Page 86—Solid, Liquid, or Gas?
1.a 2.c 3.b 4.d 5.a

Page 89—How NOT to Get Eaten
1.a 2.c 3.b 4.d 5.a

Page 92—First in a Balloon
1.d 2.c 3.b 4.a 5.d

Page 95—Why Pant?
1.d 2.a 3.a 4.c 5.b

Page 98—Maria's Comet
1.b 2.a 3.d 4.c 5.c

Page 101—The Largest Land Animal
1.b 2.c 3.a 4.b 5.d

Page 104—Raining Toads
1.c 2.b 3.a 4.c 5.a

Page 107—Hot and Cold on Mercury
1.d 2.c 3.d 4.a 5.a

Page 110—What Do You Need?
1.c 2.b 3.a 4.b 5.a

Page 113—All About Hurricanes
1.d 2.a 3.c 4.d 5.b

Page 116—Into a Crocodile's Mouth
1.c 2.c 3.b 4.d 5.b

Page 119—The Snowflake Man
1.c 2.b 3.d 4.a 5.c

Page 122—Snow on the Equator
1.c 2.a 3.c 4.a 5.b

Page 125—Flowers on the Move
1.a 2.c 3.a 4.d 5.d

Page 128—Penguins
1.c 2.a 3.b 4.a 5.d

Page 131—Mud from the Sky
1.d 2.d 3.c 4.a 5.b

Page 134—The Biggest Rain Forest
1.d 2.b 3.a 4.c 5.b

Page 137—A Lucky Accident
1.a 2.d 3.b 4.c 5.a

Page 140—The Largest Hopper
1.b 2.d 3.b 4.a 5.a

Made in the USA
Monee, IL
07 November 2022